# THE WORK THAT BRINGS PEACE IN ME

## FROM AFRICA THROUGH HATE TO LOVE— JOURNEY TO EPIPHANY

**COSTA NZARAMBA NDAYISABYE**

2012

Printed in the USA

ISBN: 978-1-938394-00-3

Library of Congress Control Number: 2012935810

*Published by:*
Great Life Press, Rye, New Hampshire 03870   USA
www.greatlifepress.com

*Cover photo*: Emily Goodman, Malibu Beach, California, USA
www.emilygoodman.com

*Back cover photo*: Carol Nazaruk Marocco, Edmonton, Alberta,
Canada   www.cmaroccoart.com

The School for The Work techniques and materials referred to
in this book may be used under the permission and guidance
of Byron Katie International. Visit the Website at
www.thework.com for more information.

The Judge Your Neighbor Worksheet is available for download
from: www.thework.com/thework-jyn.php

The book *The Work that Brings Peace in Me* was edited by Kathleen Grant in 2010. Kathleen comes from California, U.S., where she studied anthropology and sociology in her undergraduate years. Kathleen achieved her master's degree in the Social Sciences from Abo Akademi University, Finland, in 2009 and is currently a doctoral candidate in the Sociology of Education at Turku University specializing in intercultural education. She is also an English teacher and English language proofreader.

This book *The Work that Brings Peace in Me* was considerately proofread by Peter Nicholas Smyth in 2011.

Peter achieved a BFA in Drama/English, with distinction from University of Regina, Saskatchewan, Canada, in 1981; an award of professional excellence in teacher training PDP from Simon Fraser University, British Columbia, Canada, in 1987; a master of arts in directing dramatic literature from Western Washington University, Washington State, USA in 1994. Currently Peter teaches English at Okanagan College, Penticton, British Columbia, Canada, and contributes to "The One Person Project."

# Readers' Comments

"Sometimes, even when you least expect it, good can emerge from the most tragic of circumstances. Costa Ndayisabye shows that through the grassroots advocacy of forgiveness and practical reconciliation not only can damaged relations be repaired but the entirety of our humanity can be increased. His commitment to communal healing and his personal talent shines through the darkness of his past life and enriches us all." —**Mark Welch PhD,** British Columbia, Canada

"Oh, my dear Costa. You have found your way home, the home of the peace in your immovable heart. Oh, my dear Costa, thank you for showing our dear little Queen Byron a wiser, peaceful way of being through The Work and your unconditional love… I am loving you Costa, dear, dear man of peace. All ways," —**Byron Katie,** Spiritual Teacher, Byron Katie Institute, Ojai, CA

"You are light…" —**Dr. Jim Lockard,** author of *The Sacred Thinking.* CSL Simi-Valley, CA

"Your words and your presence in my life are a constantly renewing balm on my heart…" —**Isabelle Stahl**, *kindmind*, Edmonton, Alberta, Canada

"Brother Costa, I feel I know you and would love to meet you someday. Tears come when I read your words." —**Jeanette Stephens**

"Costa my friend, I will not forget your letter to me, Who said? "I" Said. Who Loves? "I" Love, Who suffers? "I" Suffer. Who is happy? "I" am happy, wow; everything is "I," lovely. You inspire the world." —**Stevens M.,** Boston, MA

"The Work works! Thinking everyday of your amazing grace, Costa. Love to you and your family." —**Katherine Munkley**

"You introduced to me to The Work of Byron Katie through *The Work that Brings Peace in Me;* I did it and found peace. I need to forgive me; I was the ground of my own sufferings. —**Stanley Yaola,** one of the First Nations community Chiefs, Canada.

# Contents

# Foreword

February 2, 2009. Fourteen days after the birth of our daughter Ashimwe (name she had at the Hospital right after her birth on January 18, 2009), a naming ceremony was organized for Ashimwe. When I was pregnant, I told Costa that we will name her Queen. He said yes! When our neighbors and friends gathered for the event, Costa told them that the child's name is Queen Byron Ashimwe. He took the time to share with them why he added the name Byron and explained to all the invitees about The Work of a peaceful lady called Byron Katie. "Her School gave me a peaceful shift," Costa said.

When Costa returned from his first session at School for The Work, I noticed that there were some changes to his life. He could not anymore argue easily with me on some of my sorrowful ideas that were affecting me "negatively" and he previously was the only person that I could share with my sorrows.

During the 1994 Tutsis' Genocide, I lost my parents, my siblings, my relatives, my friends and my community. I, my young brother Yves Claude, and my young sister Denise Ingabire, survived. I couldn't forget the long period I, and my brother Yves Claude spent during the Genocide in the ceiling hiding ourselves and when we left there we soon lost our skin and nails due to the effects of heat. Our hearts were totally broken and we couldn't believe how we became orphans just for being Tutsis.

I met Costa in 1997 and we married in 2003. He was the only one who could cry when I cried, who could hate when I hated, who could conflict with all people I conflicted with.

After he went through the inquiry process using The Work of Byron Katie, I felt much overloaded because he couldn't still help me to hate, conflict, cry, or grieve. One day he asked me, "Is hating, conflicting, and grieving bringing to us peace or stress?" I couldn't respond. He provided to me the inquiry guidance paper called "Judge Your Neighbor Work Sheet," designed by Byron Katie, to write down my sorrowful thoughts. I could hardly write some of them down. He drew a yellow card that contained the four questions and the Turnaround:

1. *Is it true?*
2. *Can you absolutely know that it's true?*
3. *How do you react, what happens, when you believe that thought?*
4. *Who would you be without the thought?*

*Then you turn the thought around.* "Let's do The Work," he said. We both practiced the inquiry process before even he was invited by Byron Katie to go to the School for The Work in Los Angeles. We were both criticizing The School for The Work and were considering it as a tool to kid with people's minds. However, at that time he was very serious and was considering The School his "pathways of Peace" I tried to go through the process and couldn't turn around my concept.

In March 2009, after his return from his second School for The Work, he became excellent and peaceful. At that time, he was inviting many friends from Europe and North America to come to experience The Work in Rwanda and Burundi.

Costa asked me, "What can be your answer if our son Gentil asks why you don't go to the place you were born?" I felt something awaken in me.

My time was there. I got the opportunity to open my mind and do The Work. I realized that I wasn't in a good temper with myself by living with those sorrowful ideas. Then, I wasn't in a good relationship with me and with God.

It was just after both of us doing The Work that we decided to be baptized and committed to live in good harmony with ourselves first.

I am motivated by, "Replace any darkness with light and concentrate with belief of forgiveness and release." (Dr. Jim Lockard, *The Sacred Thinking*).

Here is the time to get out from our fear, hunger, mistrust and revenge and live lovely for our lives so we can enjoy everything. The simple process is to question our minds. The Work is always sounding in me.

Costa became an international speaker and his transformation is the result of his peaceful trip for our entire family.

"Enjoy The Present," is Costa's dictum.

I love you Darling,
Bernadette Ndayisabye [Costa's wife]

# Preface

Friends of the Universe, during the time you are reading this book from one paragraph to another, take time to question your mind, find out if there is any stressful thought you are living with, balance and see if it is bringing in you peace or stress. As you will continue to read, you will find how our minds import stressful thoughts from the past, "Stories," which we use in our daily curriculum.

A friend of mine from a TV station in Canada asked me, "Costa, who do you think is destroying the World?" I simply replied, "I" am the one.

He also asked me, "Who do you think can make this World lovely?" I said, "I" am the one.

When I do not know the truth of my life, I always live with my stressful thoughts. When we question our stressful thoughts, we can easily come to know the truth.

I don't know which organization, family, religion, or society you come from; however, the inquiry process for every stressful moment can be indispensable, making it useful for all individuals.

When I question my mind in this manner, my vision is enlarged and I can see deep in me. I need The Work to make my life peaceful. It is therefore essential to know when I am distressed: What is the most important step that can help me to be a much more nonviolent person?

A courageous man, who is also a friend of my family, works with an international organization which provides food to refugees and to other vulnerable families. He told me about how their efforts are creating dependency among the beneficiaries. I said I would feed my mind and then my body. I always see planes carrying food, clothes, medicine to people who are victims of civil wars in Africa, my continent. It is so good to bring such help. However, it would be much better if these United Nations planes would have people like Dr. Jim Lockard, Byron Katie, Eckhart Tolle, Dr. Wayne Dyer, Pamela Grace, Bill Twist, Lynne Twist, Isabelle Stahl, Christina Syndikus, and others on board, individuals who can assist people in crisis to live "The Present" and "*Love what is*" through their spiritual teachings. I added to him that feeding the body is good, but if our minds are much more attached to what we lost because of the war and our relatives who were killed, we will need people who can help us think much more about our inner peace. *"Have a Mind That is Open to Everything and Attached to Nothing."* (Dr. Wayne Dyer)

The book relates a self-Inquiry that can help to find out the truth and then make life into something lovely from an ultimate choice.

It is now very simple for me to discover what does not go well in me and open my mind to an inquiry process. The inquiry process helps me to notice that all the events which negatively affected my life in the past should not drive my actual life today. I found that if my past experiences drive my actual life, I would live similarly to those experiences and possibly live in a state even worse than during the period that they happened. But I can now get the chance to question my mind and find what is true or even truer for my life.

Should I live The Present or the Past? Does my story bring peace or suffering/hatred?

I have frequently used my past which was full of atrocity, misfortune, and suffering that was stressfully applied to my daily life. It was obviously the past story. An internal voice will say to me, "Find the reality of your life in your story," and, I believed it. However, is what I believe true? In his book *The Sacred Thinking*, Doctor Jim Lockard of The Center for Spiritual Living, Simi Valley, California, said:

*When you make the choice to direct your thinking consciously, you step to the helm of the ship of your life and you take the wheel. Actually, you have always had the wheel, but you may have been living unconsciously, thinking of yourself as a victim, or perhaps believed that you were at the mercy of forces outside yourself. These mistaken beliefs have caused much misery but **they have never taken the wheel out of your hands!***

**It is by the process called "The Work of Byron Katie" that I managed to move from the story and go to the reality, which is "*The Present.*" That happened when I went to The School for The Work and spent nine days with Byron Katie in August 2008.**

Who is Byron Katie?

Byron Kathleen, commonly known as Katie, is married to author Stephen Michelle. Katie always gives a smile that reflects intense peace in her. She is calm sometimes—especially when she is presenting her materials. She always fixes her eyes on the person she is talking to and adopts a "listening character," and, amicably, uses fraternal words like, "Sweetheart, Honey, Angel."

Hundreds of people have described Katie and the way she inspired them in the self-inquiry process, "The Work."

My wife Bernadette, having heard of Byron Katie from my debates and workshops and having read her book *Loving What Is,* said: "Byron Katie is a leader of the Peaceful team; her job burns suffering by leaving the place to love."

My elder brother Leopold, who had the opportunity to go to The School for The Work with Byron Katie in Los Angeles, described Byron Katie as water from a rocky river. She is clear and good to hear when you're thirsty for peace.

I know a writer and friend of peace called Richard Lawrence Cohen, who was born in New York but then became *Austinate* as he uses to say, because he is now living in Austin;

he was my roommate during The School for The Work, then became a friend and is currently brother of many Rwandans. He said something on Byron Katie's personality.

In his *article* called *"I am in Love,"* this is how Richard depicts the way he saw Byron Katie. "Who Is Byron Katie?"

Funny question. I hear her replying, "The one holding this cup of tea right now," or, "Who knows?"All I can tell you is who I heard and saw. At the beginning of each day's session, without any introduction, Katie walks in and sits in a large gray easy chair on the little stage. There is a folding screen behind her, a large vase of sunflowers, and a small table with a pitcher of hot herbal tea. She appears to be in her mid-60s, about five feet five (165 cm), with short silver hair worn in bangs, and makeup. Rectangular rimless glasses come out when she needs to read something. She dresses in soft, good-quality natural fabrics, often of purple or pink-beige, and favors large shawls. Her voice is clear, direct, accentless, becoming slightly scratchy if the day has worn on. She does not seem affected in anyway. The bangs give an impish quality that balances her quiet forcefulness and occasional sternness. She smiles and laughs at the same times you or I would; she can be spontaneously funny (she can also laugh at herself, as we saw during a graduation parody performed by the staff), and she's warm when greeting individuals or groups, but she's not a smiley-face; she has serious work for us and for herself. She speaks in well-thought-out sentences, some of which sound like things she has said often before (and in many cases are familiar from her books) and which she repeats because they are, for her, bedrock truths. At other times, she says things off the cuff that are startling in their aptness. She responds readily to every question and seems unconcerned whether her answers will please us or not. —*Richard Lawrence Cohen's blog, "Writer Without a Story," (richardlawrencecohen. blogspot.com) April 29, 2007.*

There came my time to question my mind and myself—to jump into the mind-questioning process. My mind was creating a fearful resistance to the first steps of the inquiry process. That is what happens. All the time it's very painful to discover conflict and hatred that ruins our lives. If we do not keep inviting our mind to an inquiry conversation, we end up by being consumed by fear and anger. However, we have the ability to change our life to a lovely one, since peace is not something you can get from someone, from school, from a store or from a factory—it is there, inside us and we have to discover it. Just notice the ability to do so.

I realized that my being shouldn't continue to be fed by my fearful mind, and I embraced The Work that brings peace in me. Now, "whose business when I am living with stress, anger, conflict, or hatred?" The Work responded.

I invite everyone, while reading this book, to take a deep breath, get into your own self, take a moment and go with questioning interaction with the mind. Use the "I" that repeatedly appears in this book as if you are talking to yourself and see if you are really peaceful or stressful.

Costa Ndayisabye,
March 2012

# What Is "The Work"?

The Work is a simple yet powerful process of inquiry that teaches people to identify and question thoughts that cause all the suffering within us. It's a way to understand what's hurting one's self and to address problems with clarity.

The process considers four questions plus the Turnaround.

1.  *Is it true?*
2.  *Can you absolutely know that it's true?*
3.  *How do you react, what happens, when you believe that thought?*
4.  *Who would you be without the thought?*

Then you turn the thought around, once, two times, three times, as many times as you need. For example: He doesn't love me. **Turnaround**: He loves me. How? He called me and said, "Happy birthday."

Find more genuine examples for the Turnaround at *www. thework.com.*

These four questions and the Turnaround, which I exercised frequently and profoundly, showed me that the judgments I carried against other people, were harshly amplifying my own sufferings.

## Stories and Effects

By 1959 my country Rwanda had fallen into chaos. Fear developed among a group of people, full of their stories, and they turned against their fellow citizens and began killing them.

Who would have given these characteristics to the Rwandans? Was it necessary to believe the hateful ambitions said to such Rwandan brothers?

Hate purveyors said "How can you, the cultivators who represent a big number in the population of Rwanda, be dominated by this small group of stockbreeders?" They added by saying to them that these stockbreeders have physical characteristics different from those of you cultivators. The cultivators were then called Hutus and the stockbreeders were called Tutsis, and **many minds believed that**.

Hate took on its expansion, a big number of innocent Tutsis were killed in a horrible manner and other ones set off as exiles, including my father Ndayisabye Claver, who was eleven years old and my mother Mukamazimpaka Marthe, who was seven years old; their surviving families of massacres headed to Burundi.

A life of exile began, a life of suffering, begging to survive, in Burundi, a country where now-well-known tribal atrocities occurred afterwards.

In 1968 my mother Martha married Claver, both from the so-called Tutsis' ethnic group, who fled Rwanda. I was born seven years later, on July 5th.

Life in Burundi became harder and harder and my family decided to move to the Eastern part of Democratic Republic of Congo (formerly Zaïre) and now called *Uvira*. We were told several times by our parents that the reason why we are experiencing a difficult life is because we are refugees.

Reflecting on my childhood, I remember when I was six, just a few days before my father died. At the time I was studying at Munanira primary school in Uvira, Democratic Republic of

Congo. On the way back home, I picked up a nice pin badge. I did not know the person in the picture on that badge. I attached it on my school uniform shirt. It was so nice and I was proud of it. Arriving home, my father saw it and found that the man on the badge was the president of Rwanda at that time, Juvenal Habyarimana. He started stinging my ears with the pin on the badge. My ears were bleeding and my father emphasized that all suffering, starvation, and vulnerability that my family was experiencing derived from that president, Juvenal Habyarimana and "**I**" **believed that.**

I grew up knowing that there is a president in Rwanda who is causing our suffering. My mind started amplifying and storing that statement. As I was growing up, my mind continued to develop the links between the suffering of my ears and that of the president, furthermore, his ethnicity.

In 1981, my father passed away from an abrupt death when my mom was in Burundi giving birth to a new baby. He died when he was expecting to meet his first daughter, whom he had named Anitha Murekatete, *Murekatete,* meaning, "Give to her a lovely freedom."

In our house there were new baby clothes, a large quantity of rice and beans, food that father did not eat because the day before my mom came from Burundi with a new baby, he died. I had been told for many years that my father had purchased that special food for a party he was planning for our family which was going to have its first girl after five boys. My father died. My father died. My father died. He died, without completing the party he planned. He died without seeing his first daughter Anitha. He did not see her. My mind kept reminding me of that repeatedly, over and over.

Food my father purchased for the birth event of his new baby was unexpectedly served during the mourning process of his death.

I can still remember my mom's face during the mourning period, though I was very young. She was crying looking at us near the coffin where my father's body laid, with her newly bald head, which was required by Congolese culture for a wife who has lost her husband.

It was said that Helena *witched* him since she was jealous of how my father was preparing to welcome our first sister Anitha Murekatete.

A widow called Helena, a neighbor, was responsible for my father's death since he fell down and died abruptly in Helena's yard. My Uncle Callixte, who was close to my father, confirmed that. All of us were informed that Helena witched our father Claver and **we believed that.**

My paternal aunt, Anastasie Mukamana, who fled Rwanda with my father on her shoulder after losing relatives in 1959 Tutsis' massacres, fell down in a faint.

It was very sad at that time, seeing my mom holding Anitha, a four-day-old new baby, crying on the side of a wooden coffin while looking down at her dead husband.

Within my mind, I grew up thinking that Helena caused my mom to become a widow. So did my siblings who repeatedly told me to plan revenge for our dear father. What could we do as young boys? Was that a fair decision to satisfy our minds?

The life of a widow, Martha, with six children, was totally confused. She did three years of elementary school before her family fled Rwanda. She did not have any other skills, apart from buying and reselling small quantities of sugar and salt. We would rarely get to eat lunch and dinner in the same day. Although he was young, my brother Leopold was compelled to learn how to make a local metal stove at the age of eleven; I started making mud bricks during school holidays and people would pay me a small amount of money to buy school uniforms and a few exercise books.

Sometimes my mom was coerced into begging other Rwandese, our "so-called relatives" in Burundi who were in better financial positions, to assist her with small amounts of money to survive during a short period of time.

Who could pay for our school fees if we ate regularly? There was no United Nations High Commission for Refugees "UNHCR" in the Democratic Republic of Congo at that time to support desperate people who fled their country.

My mom loved us dearly. Sometimes during the night, she would tell us stories about Rwanda. She would start with tales she also learned from her parents in a refugee camp in Burundi, and end her stories in tears. I remember her saying: "We were chased out by Hutus from our beautiful country Rwanda. These Hutus are dangerous people; they do not want us Tutsis to live in Rwanda." These stories were positively welcomed by my poor mind and "**I**" **believed that.**

My mom did not see us as happy persons in the future; rather as poor ones. She knew that we were going to grow up in very hard situations. From her stressful life she was raising her children to accept a miserable life. From my experience, we Africans often believe much of what our moms tell us. Many children, "**I**" in particular, are much closer to their moms than to their fathers. **I believed everything my mom was telling us on why we were experiencing a poor, conditioned way of living.**

My siblings and I were several times advised and warned by mom to be careful with children we were making friends with. To her, our friends should be at what she believed as "The same levels like ours." Our friends should be children who were fatherless or motherless, from poor families, as she was saying, those who could only get meals once per day—children like us.

My mom was showing us that she was a very unfortunate widow in the area. She was trying to actualize the past; for her the Universe was totally her enemy; she was full of fear of both today and tomorrow and her mind was trying to reason the surrounding "children" that there were other actors causing our sufferings. "**I**" **simply believed that.**

> *If I Say, "I am unhappy," and continue to say it, the subconscious mind says, "Yes, you are unhappy," and keeps me unhappy as long as I say it, for thoughts are things, and an active thought will provide an active condition for good or evil.* —Ernest Holmes, *The Science Mind*

My mind, yet fresh at that age, was supposed to be fed on love and peace but it was totally the opposite. I was just "milking" from what my mother had in her mind.

I was warned not to make friends with a boy whose family was close to us, simply because he had both parents. That guy, Dieudonné, was just feeling the passion of being my friend. Several times he would bring us smoked fish and we would cook it at home. But the problem was that he was not allowed to be my friend because he had both parents.

When I was in elementary school I had two friends who were my classmates at the same time. One day they came to visit me, and my mom was very curious to know if they had both parents. After they responded that their mom separated with their father, my mom told me, "These are your friends since you are both in charge of your moms."

How could I know some had the same lifestyle as mine? Is it true that when we are all motherless or fatherless, it means that we have the same life situation?

There were many widows in the area where we were living in Uvira, whereby their families had a good standard of life, some even better than families with both parents. Was my mom right or was her mind trying to accentuate fear in her? After living and reviving her stories she projected them to me and to my siblings, and "**I**" **believed that.**

What happened to me? In time as I and my siblings were growing up, I started pitying my mom and living hopelessly. My brother Leopold and my younger brother Claude decided to drop out of school, crossed the Congolese border, and went to Burundi for labor. We were happy that they left since the number of children my mom was feeding decreased, even though the stories remained identical.

The stressful situation we were in made a huge negative impact on our social lives, economic status, and our education.

My mom was an excellent worker. She knew that despite all the stories, she needed to do her best to feed her family. On her head, she would carry four basins of sugar, salt, sorghum flour, and tea, four times to and from two markets per day. When these basins came back from the market empty, we were given hope that we would have food to eat. We knew all of the business went positively. But when the basins came back home with the same weight that they were taken to the market, it was horrible. We starved. Stories were brought back to my mom and the simple answer was that Helena, the presumed agent of my father's death, and the Hutus in Rwanda, were at the center of our sufferings.

What was the connection between my mom's business failure and Helena? What was the connection between her business and the Hutus who were ruling Rwanda? Her mind was just developing her negative thinking and she wanted to share it with us. My mom was fearful and expected me and my siblings to agree, and participate in the blame.

# Hopeless Created Hopeless

Despite the stories, I and my siblings are still alive.

The area where we lived was characterized by many epidemic diseases and a large number of children were not immunized. It was considered normal to hear our neighbors crying and screaming at night because a child had died. It was not strange to bury at least one person every week, most of whom were children. As teenagers, we were the ones to have to dig the tombs, and I remember in one day we could possibly dig for two people who died in one family, and much of the blame would be on the neighbors who were presumed to have witched them.

We were warned several times by our mom to never eat at our neighbors, but as children we did that clandestinely and we never felt sick. We were frequently subjected to interviews from both our mom and our aunt when we had bellyaches, head-aches, or certain problems related to our muscles. All of these were normal sicknesses. When we had a headache or bellyache my Aunt Anastasie used to take us to a so-called "*witchcraft healer*" who did nothing. We were cured after my mom got some medicines from the pharmacy.

> *What you believe comes easier than what you don't.* —Father Vincent Mulago (Zaïre)

My mind was full of beliefs, which certainly were the source of all confusions. We were told and we believed. My mind gave value to what I was told and projected it to my life.

> *Our thoughts create our mental images and beliefs… —Sacred Thinking*, by Dr. Jim Lockard

I grew up warned that:

- It was forbidden "to turn back to the graveyard when you are coming from a burial ceremony." What will happen? You will see the person you buried on your bed at night." "**I**" **believed that.**
- Never point your finger to a graveyard; your finger will steadily be deformed. "**I**" **believed that.**
- To protect your mother from giving birth to an albino, always remember to spit down onto your own chest when you see an albino. "**I**" **believed that**.
- It was very dangerous to go to the river at noon. It was the demons' time to swim in the river. "**I**" **believed that.**
- Do not cross the graveyard at noon; malicious demons will take out your mind and you will become mad. "**I**" **believed that.**
- You have to wash your hands when you come from a burial ceremony to avoid having nightmares where you can see again the dead person. "**I**" **believed that.**

All of the above thoughts were accommodated by the mind. Were they bringing stress within me, or peace? My mom told me that she did not look back when leaving the graveyard after burying my father. We needed to be careful with anything that concerned death, my mom added.

In her book *Question Your Thinking, Change the World*, Byron Katie said:

*No one knows what's good and what's bad. No one knows what death is. Maybe it's not a something; maybe it's not even a nothing. It's the pure unknown, and I love that. We imagine that death is a state of being or a state of nothingness, and we frighten ourselves with our own concepts....*

What was told is totally what was in all people's minds. Too many of my people conceptualized their fear and wanted generation after generation to believe the same; in other words, to live fearfully.

This is what most of the children will be learning from their parents when the latter are attached to their stressful stories. A child with a fresh mind will get primary thoughts from the parents. If their minds are full of hatred, children's minds will be hateful consequently; if parents' minds rely on stories, consequently their children might rely on that, if parents are full of love, they will have lovely children.

I came to realize that the life we were experiencing was not so critical. I suffered from *kwashiorkor.* The Encyclopedia Britannica defines kwashiorkor as *a "severe malnutrition in infants and children especially of impoverished regions caused by a diet low in protein."* My mom was compelled to go to Burundi from the Democratic Republic of Congo where we were living, to solicit financial support from her "so-called relatives," and spent one month there. At that time we were left at our aunt's home. It was its time to visit my body and was a time of challenge.

*If you believe that you are "not enough," you will validate that belief and create the reality that you don't have enough. But if you believe that you are more than enough, you will create more than enough in every part of your life*—H.Eker

Since we were living hopelessly there was nothing positive that our minds could believe or commit to do. Hope did not get placed in our lives at that time, yet it could be the most necessary tool for us to live contently.

> *…hope generates hope. All contributions and success build and feed in a cyclical fashion into the very production and fostering of that one most necessary element of life: hope. Therefore, hope not only becomes nourishment for the whole, it is also a by-product available to the many…* —*Creative in Struggle* by Twilla R. Welch

Hopeless creates hopeless. It happened to my mom's mind, fearfully deciding to forge our names so that they could be confused as Congolese names. Arbitrarily the Congolese Inspector of Education in Uvira, where we were living, decided to double school fees for all Rwandans. We were very fearful with that decision and the only solution my mom saw was to transform our names. My names Ndayisabye Nzaramba Costa were therefore changed to Ndaïsabie Zaramba Costa. Added on that, we were told to tell everyone that we were Zaïrians (current Congolese). I and my siblings started to spread the news that we were not Rwandans, rather Zaïrians from a Rwandan mom.

Some people could easily believe that we were Zaïrians especially young ones; however, that did not last for long because when I had to sit for the national exam that ended my high school studies, I changed again my names to original ones on the registration form so that they could appear on my diploma and there arose troubles and my mom had to sell her goat for me to give a bribe to the Inspector of Education. I passed and on my diploma my names appeared as my father named me. What were we doing? What were our minds dealing in?

We had a long way to go, but where to? The place was unknown. We had already spoiled our vision by relying on our past and "*living with our stories.*"

I remember when I finished the first level of high school; I was very devoted to embrace math and physics sections, but my mom advised me to do the teacher training school "*Humanités Pédagogiques.*" What was the reason behind that choice? What was the reason to be a future teacher in the Democratic Republic of Congo? Teachers were rarely and badly paid. They got a narrow incentive from students' parents, which was worth less than US$10 per month.

My mother's choice relied on the fact that teachers got much money from selling marks to students. It was easy to buy the exam questionnaires with answers from a teacher. My mom saw in me a very good "income yielder" of my family if I would be a teacher. "**I**" **believed that.**

All these did not have anything to do with truth, with hope, with peace, but rather were sowing stress and creating a crop of failure.

I was breastfeeding hatred, fear, and stories, which were characterizing my life.

I was the first child in my family to be put in jail three times in three countries. I used to call this a curse. I always thought I was cursed by God. My mom told me several times that I needed to go to an intercession room so that pastors could pray for me.

When you give much value to your thoughts it will conduct or misconduct your life. So it is much more necessary to try not to let your blind mind guide your life. If so, you will be like "trash" and you will contain everything your mind will put in you.

Stories create hatred when they bring you a stressful past in the present moment. They cause anger and vengeance. Revenge is always blind.

I had down pat what my mom did to me.

One day I came from school at 1 pm and I was really hungry. I was in primary school in grade 5. My mom was not there and we had to wait until she came back from the market at 3pm so that we could make our daily lunch, "cassava paste." It was very normal that we did not eat anything in the morning and waited for that late lunch. However, we had some fish in our saucepan and were waiting for cassava paste. My mind told me to find where the saucepan was so I could get a temporary remedy for my hunger. I looked around, making sure that my brothers did not follow my movements. I opened the saucepan, got a stew of fish and ate it. It was a taboo to go in the saucepan or to grab food somewhere in a house without the permission of the one who was responsible for that. It could be worse if the homeowner was another person other than your parents or relatives.

When my mom came and found that the fish was eaten she called us, and I was the only one found with a soup spot on my shirt. She asked me furiously why I dared to open the saucepan. I did not have anything to say, I was just crying. The punishment was expected to be tough. The first was to imme-diately be excluded from among those who were going to have lunch. Then I had to starve and wait for the coming day at 3pm to get food. The second punishment was much worse. It was considered as merciless for years and years. She crushed red pepper and put it in my eyes. On that heartless action she added some strong and hateful words, "You are an orphan and you must resist hunger."

When I started losing my breath because of screaming, my mom, who planned and implemented that punishment, also started running amok, washing my face and putting mother's milk, "maternal milk" in my eyes. Did she do that to satisfy her concern about the consequences of the piece of fish I ate? Did that bring peace in her or stress? Was that an appropriate cure or punishment for a child like me who was truly hungry?

Most of the time our minds will create things that will constitute horrible behavior pretending that the latter will bring peace. Here and there children in Africa are tortured by their parents accusing them of getting food from the saucepan without permission.

When I was working with World Vision in Nyamata, Rwanda, a lady who was full of stressful stories due to a poor relationship with her husband burned her nine-year-old daughter because she grabbed one sweet potato from the pot when her mom wasn't there.

At the age of seventeen years, I was put in jail by a Congolese soldier (Zaïrian soldier at that time). He was our neighbor and sometimes a very lovely old man. Most Congolese soldiers at that time were paid erratically. After seven to eleven months their salary could come and they might only get one or two months of their arrears. Rwandan refugees were mostly acting as victims and their properties, such as domestic animals, bikes, and wheelbarrows, were periodically confiscated by Congolese militaries to forcibly pay for the poor political system of their country. Rwandan youth in particular, were the most targeted and arbitrarily arrested, beaten, tortured, and jailed.

Here was the way I found myself for the first time in jail after getting into trouble with Congolese soldier Major Sergeant Pongo, whose family was living next to our home. The day before I was arrested I was totally sick, stricken by malaria. I could not go to the hospital because we could not find treatment money. My mom bought some tablets for me from the market without a medical prescription. I was very sick. Youth from my church came to visit and pray for me. Among them came Sergeant Pongo's daughter Nema. When she stepped in to our compound, her older sister Euphrasie came and started beating her. She was accused of making friends with Rwandans.

The following day around 5:30 am, when I was waiting for my young brothers to carry me to the river Kalimabenge to wash me, Sergeant Pongo's son Ferdinand suddenly came and told me to not go anywhere. While I was asking why, two soldiers sent by Sergeant Pongo took me to the military jail known as "*Corps de garde.*" With their guns they carried me because I was really sick and could not walk. My mom started crying and saying, "My son is taken in the same way Jesus was taken."

Join me to ask myself this question, "Who reminds/tells me that I have to be angry, when I am insulted, when I feel being hated, being rejected, and so on?"

"What and who causes me to think if I am beaten, my arm, leg, or some bone are to be broken, I will die, that this will be the end of my life?"

These types of questions always find in me their ground to play and I can be the referee if I am committed to being so.

When I was put in jail I was suffering from malaria, shivering and having a resistant headache, and I believed that was the end of my life and could even imagine myself a dead person whose body would be found in jail. Fearfully, my mind believed that way.

I spent three months in a very bad jail. No windows, very poor hygienic conditions, no toilet, hundreds of thousands of cockroaches and lice that were biting me days and nights. I was released three months later after a long negotiation between Major Sergeant Pongo, who also arrested Pastor Sergeant Gahungu, a Rwandan clandestinely working for the Congolese army. I benefited from Pastor Sergeant Gahungu's advocacy since he knew my family was Rwandan. Sergeant accepted to free me with the condition that my mom had to provide one of the two goats we had at home. The goat was provided to Sergeant Pongo and he sent the order to the jail's guards to release me. The jail's guards laid me down and bludgeoned me fifty times. They were saying, "We can't free this Rwandan without teaching him the discipline that he has to pay to Congolese."

The goat was given to Sergeant Pongo who sent us some meats after slaughtering it. My mom resisted cooking that meat but accepted it when we all said that we needed it.

I don't think that the reason these soldiers maltreated me was because they were not paid their salaries. Their minds were directing their lives and were full of hatred and fear. No time to think twice was in their minds before they acted fiercely like that. Were Rwandans the root cause of their sufferings? Were Rwandans allowed or sent by their government to commit atrocities? **The guards' minds did that.** They were implementing what they believed.

At the same age of seventeen, I was also arrested and detained in Burundi, accused of being a Congolese street boy. At that time, students under eighteen years were compelled to show their student cards to cross the Democratic Republic of Congo border to Burundi. I was going there with my friend Mastaki to buy clothes for his baptism. Despite showing my student card, I was arrested. The policeman who arrested me was well known in Burundi, especially by Congolese. He was known as an infamous kidnapper, torturer, who was working with a strong Department of Municipal Police.

My friend Mastaki, who looked younger than me, was released though we were both the same age. I was taken to jail. Oh my gosh!!! What a jail! It looked like an abandoned house. I was the youngest inmate compared to the others. The first thing that happened was the prisoners shaved my hair in a very funny style. No choice, I had to be humble. They asked me to provide money for buying candles since there was no electricity there. I did not have even a coin. Therefore, according to their illegal laws, I was ordered to slap the wall with my palms fifty times for each. At the time I was detained there, that small jail, commonly known as Sobekov, was characterized by a musty smell due to horrible hygienic conditions. Windows were on one side of the wall, which was very hot during the day and cold at night. All prisoners used the bathroom twice per day at the same time, 6 am and 6 pm respectively; otherwise we employed buckets inside the jail room. We ate once per day at 5 pm. Food was brought in old nylon made bags from the main prison. When the vehicle carrying the bags came, all the prisoners shouted to welcome the food.

On my second day in that jail, the guy who arrested me came into the jail, called me and said, "With your palms slap the wall two hundred times before I release you."

I replied "Yes" dreadfully, but could not slap even twenty times. I did eighteen times and my throbbing hands turned red.

He said, "You failed and you are remaining with one hundred seventy-two times." He went away with two other prisoners from our group and the rumor was that they were going to be killed.

That policeman, who passed away in 1997 from HIV and AIDS, was fully conducted by his mind and stories. I do not think that beating, torturing, and kidnapping were the ways to make peace in him. Peace cannot be found by maltreating others. Cruelty is what we turn to when we are full of fear and our minds look for revenge, to show the "outside" that we are strong. On whose business was that municipal policeman to be fierce like that? Who was suffering? His mind was.

I was released when the police inspection exercise came after two and half months and found me there almost dead from sickness. I was suffering from malaria without any treatment. The police inspector, fearful of my health status, told me to leave the jail premises. It was 2 pm and I had to walk four hours to get back home in Uvira, Congo. I staggered that journey, very sick, because I did not have any other choice.

When I reached home in the evening around 9 pm, my mom, who thought that I had been kidnapped, was very happy to see me. She was crying and repeated the words, "*Unafufuka, unafufuka mtoto wangu*" meaning "You are resurrected, you are resurrected my son." I was very sick that time and screaming from my painful hands full of bumps and wounds. That evening, she gathered us and told us that Helena who witched our father caused all the suffering, including my two detentions. She went further and told us that Rwandan Hutus were the source of our sufferings. **I believed that**.

I was very much full of hatred and fear for tomorrow's life. What I was breastfeeding from my mom was stuck in my mind and this was unfairly driving my life.

When you are living with hatred and fear you are separated from the Truth. I could not believe that what happened, happened because it happened. There was no choice of enjoying the life we were in. Day and night were characterized by expressions of grief. We were thinking we were the only family that was experiencing the worst lifestyle.

I remember, despite all those life systems we were *swimming* in, we liked attending church services. At the age of twelve I knew the biblical verse, which said:

> *Therefore, I tell you, do not be anxious about your life, what you will eat or what you will drink, nor about your body, what you will put on. Is not life more than food and the body more than clothes?* —Matthew 6:25

This did not mean anything to us. Reading a Bible was not connected to any understanding. On the top came what our minds were vibrating for. "You are suffering; your tomorrow is totally unknown and fuzzy." So our life was fearful.

Despite having left the house where we lived near Helena, the so-called agent of our father's death, any night movement took our attention. Owl screams and night winds perturbed our lives. Nightmares were our nightly mind meals and they were getting darker and darker.

My mind was totally occupied in confusion, horror, and terror. I could not think of the distant future, my vision was so short. I just wanted to have a father close to me so that I couldn't see my mom again with that status of a refugee, widow, miserable lady. I was feeling so bad when my mom was telling me how we could grow in such a situation while being in exile. She couldn't decide to go back to Rwanda where she would bicker about the possibility that we could be killed. There was no choice; it was our moment to live as it was.

I grew up with my mind full of hatred and internal conflict. Consequently that was the experience I carried with me in my mind.

I was "throwing flowers" to my fearful mind, honoring it by believing my stories. Worries were characterizing my life. At school and in my neighborhood I was not confident of who I was. Often our minds create worry and deliver confusion.

I accepted as true that other people who could not be under my control victimized my relatives and me.

We sometimes think and want people to behave the way we want. However, they are what they are and can't be under our control. We have the ability to control ourselves—not others, though our minds keep alerting us that a certain person has to behave this way or that way for us to get peace. One might say to oneself: "He needs to say 'sorry,' she needs to live with me, she needs to hear me . . . ." We may always think that other people spoil our life and they are causing miserable situations for us.

> *Not one of us has the ability to control another. It is quite impossible. I can control myself. If I believe that I have the ability to control another I am in miserable situation. I can't even control Malachi [his one-month-old grandson].* —Pastor Stearns Philip Sr.

At times, I was living so detached it led to estrangement. I dimly sketched upon the dark background of my dreams the imperfect lineaments of the awful future that I couldn't even see. That was the confusion that I was swimming in, and I started imagining that I was the most unfortunate child in my family. Sorrowfulness was the strongest of my characteristics and my mom was impatient with my behavior at that time. Since my childhood, I did believe my mom's concept that we were cursed and couldn't get a peaceful life. That was what I got from her and my mind believed that.

We were not the only ones in that area, Uvira, Democratic Republic of Congo, who were suffering, though others' sufferings were not the source of our sufferings. Suffering was much more individual, created by what my mind believed.

One day from Radio Burundi we had a very instructive broadcasted tale and all of us were there. From my mother up to our youngest child, we all surrounded our little black radio, listening to the tale. I was happy to hear it.

*The tale was about a woman who wanted to commit suicide by drowning in the lake. The reason, which pushed her to think this way, was that she was condemned by many people because she did not have any children after twenty years of marriage. Her sisters-in-law were the first to censure her.*

In most of the Sub-Saharan African countries it is common for the husband's family to be more involved in household affairs than the wife's family. And when the issue concerns not having children, they tend to consider that as a serious problem and will blindly blame the woman.

*The woman decided to "leave the world" since she found that she was useless to her family and to this world as a whole and to her husband in particular.* Her mind advised her, *"You should give peace to these people by committing suicide."* In the evening she went to the lake to drown herself.

Sometimes we think and believe that we have duties of pleasing others. We feel guilty for a circumstance that we do not have a solution for. Our mind is there to alert us for the good and the bad. Unfortunately we often believe everything in our minds without even taking the time to meditate and scrutinize the facts.

*While she was preparing to accomplish her commitment, another woman came to the lake, devastated by her own mind and met the first one there. Eager to know, the first woman asked the newcomer why she was so upset and what did she come to do at the lake at that time.*

*Full of sadness, whimpering, she replied, "I am here to commit suicide. I have many children and they do not give me peace, just troubles. I am now disappointed. Slowly the first lady started real-izing that having children does not necessarily mean that one has peace! She was in confusion since she got the challenge of her mind from another person. The second lady asked the first lady why she was astounded. She said, "I came here to end my life, because I do not have any children." The second woman decided to stop her so-called way "to make peace," and went back home, because she was made to realize that there are women who are suffering from not having children. They both decided to go to enjoy the situations that they had.*

Both of these women expected to have peace from outside—the idea that not having or having children could make their life peaceful—their failure to have peace led them to attempt to commit suicide! Each one helped the other to do the inquiry. The story continued:

*At the same time as when the first two ladies were going back to their homes, a third woman running toward the lake found them cheerfully chatting. They told her to come down. The third woman said that she was very annoyed about what was happening to her in her family. She said that she was mistreated by her family because of not being married. Several times her relatives told her, "You are forty-five years old, you need to get married." They were telling this to her days and nights and she was feeling so guilty because she did not have a husband. In her mind, the solution for this problem was to leave this world.*

*While she was explaining to the two women, a fourth woman came to the lake. She was screaming loudly and full of tears. She stopped where the others were standing. They took her on the sand and told her to tell them what happened. She said, "What I have seen in my life is the most horrible situation anybody has experienced. I married my husband ten years ago. He loved me just from our wedding up to a few months later. Since then I am mistreated, beaten, and hated by him. He does not love me at all. We are living like enemies, yet we had very wonderful moments in our wedding and vowed to live forever lovingly, but today it is the opposite. Lucky are girls who decide to live without husbands."*

*The third young woman saw that these women were having a hard time being married! She might be better off remaining single, without a husband. She decided to share her experience with the fourth woman, telling her how she was mistreated and blamed by her family because she was not married.*

The third woman's explanation was at the same time helping the fourth woman to go deep into herself and start the inquiry. She was noticing that her decision of turning toward suicide was irrelevant.

*The fourth woman noticed that there were some people who were persecuted by their families because they were not married. She decided that it was better to have a so-called "malicious" husband instead of no husband at all.*

What can we learn from this instructive tale? Not one of the four managed to achieve her "commitment." We sometimes suffer from our own fear and feeling guilty about a circumstance. Is committing suicide a very peaceful way to solve our problems or to end our sufferings? Is it right to consider that committing suicide can bring peace to those people that our mind used to tell us are our enemies? From the inter-inquiry among the ladies they found that their decisions were very inappropriate. I knew that on several occasions when my mom said that she was suffering a lot when trying to feed us, to pay for school fees, clothe us, and so forth, that she was considering committing suicide.

I myself experienced how we think to get peace if we "leave" this world. We fearfully think we will find peace in the other world after death. It is very difficult to prove that peace was in the past or peace can be found beyond this life we are living in. Our fearful mind tells us that we are suffering and need to find peace somewhere else. I always find this like denying my individuality.

In 1985, my late Aunt Anastasie decided to commit suicide because a medical checkup revealed that she had cancer. She pounded a batch of tablets; put them in water and drank. When she started losing her mind, she started screaming and asking for mercy from God. She was rushed to the hospital and later recovered.

I considered committing suicide when I was imprisoned in Rwanda.

Hatred and fear were characterizing my life. My lovely girlfriend Bernadette, who later became my lovely wife, was with me when I was arrested by the police. She suffered tremendously, even more than me. The prison where I was jailed was located in the area where she had survived the 1994 Tutsis' Genocide. People who killed her siblings and her mother were in that prison. It was stressful for me to be among people who committed Genocide. I knew already that I was going to share the same life in jail with those who stoned and killed my wife's mother. I was thinking it was only the way to death. My mind was telling me many negative things that could happen to me while being with those prisoners. I was totally confused.

When the jail door opened for me to enter, my mind reminded me to say "*Yesu*" meaning Jesus. Everyone was very curious to see who was coming to join them on their unknown journey. It was evening and some of them could not easily move from one room to another and waited until morning to come to tell me very encouraging words, "You came just to count the windows," meaning that I would not spend a long time there.

My first night was challenging. I got a wonderful mind challenger from a guy I myself put in jail when I was working as the district police judicial inspector just one year before I was arrested. The man came with a big cup full of yoghurt and gave it to me. I was so hungry and gripped by fear that I could not tell anyone that I needed food. Fortunate as I was, I got milk from a man I might have hurt. My mind was convincing me how guilty I should feel for having arrested that man in the past and shamefully I was touched when he gave me that cup of milk. Feeling how much I was guilty about that person, I did not know why he gave me that cup of milk! The guy had moved out of his past and was full of love. He was much more living in "The Present" and didn't want to relive his past experience.

Inside, my mind was just trying to weaken me and make me sound noncommittal, undependable. Fearful vibrations and goose bumps were part of my life at that moment.

I was in the waiting room inside the prison when the group leader of the prisoners sent someone to look for me in my temporary prison cell for that night. The leader reminded me how milk is a very symbolic drink in Rwandan culture. I knew that and was very touched since I was very much attached to my culture. A Rwandan will honor his visitor by giving him or her milk. In all Rwandan weddings the bride's parents will give the groom milk to show him that they are very happy and honor him.

I found everyone very humble and disciplined in the prison and noticed that Rwandan prisoners were very kind, everyone at the same level. Priests, pastors, degree holders, non-educated, all, together, were kind. One of them told me that, "Our kindness is due to what most of us committed: Genocide." They were suffering a lot from their guiltiness. I learned a great deal about forgiveness when I was there. Contrary to my thinking, I treated them like relatives and learned some skills, such as playing guitar, composing songs, and even sharpening my English.

Oh My God! Where is peace actually peace? We try to find different ways to discover where peace is. Some will be narrating that peace was in the past; others asserting the need to fight today to find peace; one of the Latino American chief geurrillas said, "Peace is on the top of a gun." Others will say peace is in money, a beautiful house, nice clothes, children, husband, wife, and so on. Yes! If it could be true!

Saturday was a challenging day of my life in that prison. People with relatives or friends in jail had permission to visit them on Saturdays and my lovely Bernadette came to jail, respecting that appointment. I spent there 52 weeks and got 52 visits from her. She had to travel four hours each way every Saturday to come visit me. Those who killed her siblings and mom could not go outside until they knew that she had left. That made her "comfortable" because she did not want to see them. Both parties were full of trauma. The mind will tell you that avoiding eye contact with the one you hurt, or the one who hurt you, is a perfect way to make peace.

I was very ashamed of my prison uniform although its color was one of the most preferable ones in the world: Pink. The reason I was ashamed was that people might think that I committed Genocide. I was giving many projections to the outside, which was just amplifying my fear. I always told Bernadette not to come for visits since I knew she would suffer a lot when she saw me in the same "bay," in the same uniform as those who killed her siblings and her mom, those who destroyed their houses and slaughtered their cows. She kept telling me that next week she was not going to come, but it was also difficult for her and, remarkably, she came to visit me every week.

Every day in prison was the beginning of my life in prison.

December 25, 2000, a Seventh-day Adventist Pastor was scheduled to preach. I felt that it was directly about me!!! We did not know each other before, but what he taught touched my heart. My mind started realizing that there was a reason for me to be in prison. In his teaching he said that there was no one who was innocently arrested. He added, "Aren't there any other worse things you have committed clandestinely, which, once known, might even put you in jail for life?" We suddenly looked at each other! I started doing my review and saw how much I had hurt other people.

For example, back in 1997, I met Helena our "famous enemy," as my mother always was telling us and we believed she was. We siblings considered her as the one who witched my father. We met in the Central Market of Bujumbura Burundi. Full of anger and hatred, I pushed her and she fell down. Two policemen came and as I was full of revengeful spirit, I shouted, crying, "She witched my father!"

The policemen detained me for two hours; when I explained enough that they thought I was right, they released me. I felt that it was a good opportunity to make Helena pay back "the death of my father."

Several times, I had attempted to find Sergeant Pongo for retribution for how he caused me suffering by arbitrarily detaining me in the worst condition where I almost died in jail from malaria.

I had falsely hated all Hutus several times because I knew that they were the ones who committed the Genocide from 1959 up to 1994. Big and fiercely spirited pressure had given me a large selection of headaches when I was arbitrarily jailed.

I was accused of detaining people arbitrarily when I was working with the Judiciary Inspection Department of Rwanda and one of them was a guy called Gasana who was really sick.

The education was there in the prison where I had fearfully harvested a good relationship and at the same time a big challenge to my belief. I was having a feeling of guilt in my heart though at the same time my mind ominously felt innocent.

### Oh! My mind, I love the way we interact

*Oh! My mind, I love the way we interact,*
*You calmly tell me how to act,*
*You want me to believe that,*
*My dear mind I cannot believe everything you tell me,*
*Even though I know you always want peace in me.*
*I tried and I try to support you my mind,*
*What happened? What happens? That was/is not so kind?*
*I have suffered! I suffer! When you remind.*
*The Universe is what it is! Full of happiness,*
*Oh! My mind, do not act with Fearfulness.*
*Where is truth that I can live with?*
*Let us seize this moment for interaction,*
*In order to find a truthful impaction,*
*Let's use the past to make love,*
*And peacefully take sorrow and rise above,*
*Oh! My mind, I love the way we interact.*

After 52 weeks I was then released from captivity. When I was called by my name, I suddenly decided to go to see one of the prisoners, a Presbyterian church pastor, to pray for me. He asked blessings for me to behave like a Christian, by forgiving those who hurt me, to ask for forgiveness from those I hurt, to enjoy my new life, and to be protected from any kind of *"Satanic attacks."* I was very anxious on how I was going to be looked upon in the society outside of the prison.

Many hugs from my prisoner friends were just letting me experience a wistful heart. While I was going to miss them, at the same time my prisoner's status was finished. My mind fell in a deep bewilderment and didn't know what I could do. Prisoners were then like my family members and I enjoyed sharing with them different skills, talking about religions, and other different socio-cultural issues that relatively connected us. When the idea "*I am in prison*" resurfaced in my mind, I just looked around myself and saw thousands of men and women in another room who could smile and enjoy "their present life" so I resolved to drop my anger. I felt I was really going to miss them.

Then the fear was about tomorrow. My mind was attacking me and told me many perplexing ideas. Being imprisoned seemed to be a curse. *Who said that, actually said that? Who experienced that?* It was just said, customized and "**I**" **believed!**

There was one community in the Democratic Republic of Congo (formerly Zaïre), that believed, "*Once you are released from jail, you need to go wash in the river early morning before even anyone else washed. That could clear all curses and make you become a new person,*" and all the community members believed that. I had many friends from that community and sometimes I was complying with their beliefs. The question was: from which proof was my confirmation relying on? The "**I**" has this mind that what it receives from a friend has a higher percentage of accuracy. A "No" would always be hidden during conversation with my friends, my father, my mother, my brother, my sister, my husband, my wife and girlfriend.

The "**I**," minimizes the potential force that I received when I entered this lovely universe and fearfully creates a distorted way of seeing things.

I had to leave the prison anyway. The door was open and a crowd of prisoners bid me "*bye, bye, bye.*" Their voices echoed. I recall some of them saying "*Remember to come for a visit.*" I could not see properly, my sight was limited. When I approached the clerk's office for signing out I saw my young brother Didier.

Didier, my young brother, produced a beaming smile and with a big hug he said in Swahili *Mungu asifiwe,* "praised is God." I could not take much time to meditate on that; I felt strange and my eyes were looking here and there to see who was looking at me, and at the same time looking back to see my one-year home left behind—I cried!—The distance separating the prison from my mother's home was a two-hour bus ride on a hardly-drivable, muddy, bumpy road. Every person in my family and some friends were curiously waiting. A goat was slaughtered for my release and a party planned. But the party did not take place.

I, and my young brother Didier missed the bus.

Early morning the following day, we took the bus and I was happy to see the prison again as we drove by it; I slowly raised my hand and waved at the building. I could not talk much though my young brother was trying to ask me some questions. As we were approaching my mother's home I could not even summon courage to greet people. My mother saw me and tears poured out of her eyes; she hugged me and said *Mungu asifiwe* "Praised is the Lord."

Days and days passed and I did not know what to do. People were trying to come to visit me and I avoided meeting most of them except a few who had come to see me when I was in jail.

My mind wrongly did selection and told me that, *It is when you are in a difficult time that you know who your friend is.* I thought no one was compelled to be my friend. Much more so, visiting someone in jail, in a hospital, is not a friendship indicator. These were the prejudiced aspects that my mind was fearfully forcing me to utilize and "**I**" **believed that.**

As the days passed, I accumulated anger and hatred in me. I adopted this as the new way to live. I was living in a purely selfish way and forgot the connection that people are part of the Universe. My anger was amplified and I could not control that. I was wondering if I was born to be jailed in different prisons. I hated some of the people who were calling me "*Mandela.*" My brother called me CEPGL "*Great Lakes Countries Economic Community*" because I was jailed in The Democratic Republic of Congo, Burundi, and Rwanda, the countries which formed that community. I got angry with him and stopped speaking to him.

> *When you say "I am anxious," you become anxious. That is the way you choose to be anxious. When someone is anxious, he always makes mistakes. I can advise you to choose peace. Do not choose peace by force. Meditate and learn how to go for good choice.*
> —Pastor Stearns Philip Sr.

My life was then obscure, full of ambiguities, with no clear way forward since I was living with a whole host of bad stories that were forcibly guiding my mind.

I was very isolated and thought myself useless. My mother was very close to me; she knew I was very angry. I had a persistent cough and I was taken to the hospital for a medical check; however, nothing was disclosed. The doctor said to my mother that my cough was due to the change of food and atmosphere. That was the doctor's assumption and my mind, on the other hand, started to count the people who died after leaving the prison and I imagined I was facing the same situation.

I stayed in a small dark room where it was difficult to tell night from day. My mind was still in "Jail." I decided then to write to God on how I had been suffering all my life. I wanted him to intervene and to not be unresponsive towards the difficult moments I was passing through. I thought and believed my peace was not in me. More so, I believed the Congolese *assumption*, which speculated that *every person is born lucky but that luck can be taken away at any time by devils.* I therefore decided to write to God!

*God,*

*Why did you create me? Why did you want*
*me to be in this "Crazy World"?*
*Since I was born, I have never had peace.*
*Only sufferings and sufferings!*
*Where did my Destiny go? Who took it?*
*Whom shall I be without my Destiny?*
*I could not imagine the way my life would be!*
*Other boys and girls of my age grew up with*
*their destiny and are enjoying it,*
*They had benefited from strong affection*
*from their parents you protected,*
*I got hatred instead from an unfortunate widow,*
*who innocently lost her husband,*
*Who did, herself, hardly believe in our survival and our growth!*
*My life was spoilt from the worst past*
*experiences, that left in me suffering.*
*I was, several times, a victim of torture in*
*Democratic Republic of Congo.*
*Why did you leave me? Why did you*
*indifferently look at my sufferings?*
*In all the three jails I have been put in, I was calling you for help.*
*Now I am lost on the Road of Life! I am so sad*
*and quiet sitting in total confusion,*
*Who is going to bring peace in me? You*
*are the one, God, to solve this!*
*I want to get my destiny back. Allow me*
*to enjoy what others are enjoying.*
*I was not born to explore jail's life. Enough! I felt weak!*
*Oh! My God! Tell me what you think for me to become peaceful.*

*I feel disappointed and sad, sad and abandoned.*
*It is your time to act and change my life to a peaceful one.*
*My heart is hurting and my eyes are stinging.*
*Oh! My God! Don't just understand my*
*complaints: rather act positively;*
*If you did not curse my life, why can't you say "No" to my misery?*
*If you did curse me, it is time to forgive me, to wash my misery.*
*Allow me to have a new peaceful and lucky life!*

# CHAPTER 3

# Was My Peace There?

When the "I" believes misguidedly in its fearful mind, it will always start blaming the outside "surrounding" and portray it as the source of suffering. Is it true someone is, or was, assigned to this World to suffer? Our minds can convince us repeatedly that: my mother hates me, my father does not care for my life, I was abandoned by my family, God does not understand my prayers, and so forth.

Ironically, in the same way "I" was blaming others for being responsible for my sufferings, I also believed that they were willing to help me find my peace.

I was emphatically expecting to be given peace from people, and from God. That is why I felt hatred toward everybody, except my mother and my fiancée Bernadette.

After six months spent in a room in my mother's house sleeping, crying, grinding my teeth, and sometimes contemplating suicide, I was mentally sick and basically incapable of meeting many people. I thought being isolated was one of the ways to find peace. My friend Meschak, who likes to tell jokes, came several times to joke and I could sometimes smile but, inevitably, after he left I wallowed in my grief. I had a persistent headache, and a cough, which got worse at night, despite taking medication my mother bought from the pharmacy and receiving what comforts Bernadette brought me. I could spend four hours screaming during the night.

Bernadette found a job for me in Nyamata. I was assigned to work with orphans and other vulnerable children in the area.

I decided to marry Bernadette because she was what brought forth my feelings of compassion and love. I was monitoring the children's education, social and health status; some of them were fatherless or motherless, some complete orphans, while some had one or both parents in jail.

Bernadette, who was at that time my fiancée, always told me that she was ready to help terminate my anger and sorrows. She kept insisting that we make an official wedding. I was lucky to marry her. Our wedding, comprised of a very small number of people compared to other African weddings, was then completed. Some of the "so-called" friends and relatives teased me for having done a wedding in a small truck. We had used, of course, my brother's friend's small truck when the newly-weds, I and my wife, went back home from the wedding place. We did not have a choice; we had no money to hire comfortable cars! On the whole it was unusual for many people's standards around the world but our wedding target was achieved. "*Wedding doesn't mean nice car at all, it means what I want it to mean.*"

Bernadette had some uncles and cousins who survived the Rwandan Tutsis' Genocide, who could not participate in the wedding because she was marrying a "cursed person." They did not want me to marry her at all. They had even told me several times that I should not dare to engage with her. However, the wedding was then completed. We did not think much about the video that was taken because of the quality of our wedding, which was unfortunate. I felt ashamed to show my friends or my future children that humble wedding and I decided to burn the videotape.

When you are living stressfully, you are living mistakenly. You believe negatively and do things that are not peace compliant. I used to say, "That's amplifying your sadness."

I decided not to participate in weddings because mine was a wretched one. At my job, I was not providing proper affection to children who were living despondently. I was working for being paid and not to render the service I was assigned to. I knew those orphans and other vulnerable children were in a very difficult situation and needed love, but they could not get from me what I did not have. My mind rebelled against myself. Anytime when I met those children, I used to tell them that they were not suffering since they had some people, the organization, catering to their lives. And on the other hand, I was like a "Mentor"! But, due to the upheaval in my mind, I was in a way "encouraging" their trauma and stress, targeting the last day of the month for my salary. Bluntly, that is what I had *and that is what I was giving to those innocent children.*

I remember one day I went for a visit to a family whose father was in jail accused of having participated in the 1994 Tutsis' Genocide. The mother of the family revealed how much she was suffering to feed six children as well as visiting her husband once per month. "*It is too hard for me, to prepare food for my vulnerable children and prepare to visit my husband where he is in Jail. It is a long way to go and I walk all day long one-way,*" she told me.

I was very angry with that and considered her as someone who was happy with what her husband did.

*Was that true?* I furiously told her that all those miseries they were experiencing were due to what her husband did during the Tutsis' Genocide and they needed to payback. *Was that true?* Her children were right there when I was saying that. That is the fruit of my stressful mind.

Hatred and conflict were part of my life. Time after time I was getting an alarm from my mind that I should think about what happened to me, why it all happened, and what I could do with those facts, which spoiled my life. I was suffering intensely by being deeply connected to my past.

But when I embraced The Work, the curtain that was blocking my inner peace became transparent.

> *Nothing is more important than when we confront the appearance of difficulty, loss, sadness, and grief.* —Dr. Jim Lockard, CSL Simi Valley

## ✃ CHAPTER 4 ✃

# Connection with The Work

Friday evening July 20, 2007, I received a phone call from a number, which was not familiar to me. The voice was very soft, peaceful and slow;

> *My name is Marion MacGillivray, I am with my husband Keith and my daughter Genevieve. We are Americans; we are here in Rwanda for a visit and would like to meet you. We got your phone number from your Canadian friend Carrie.*

I replied to them that I knew Carrie, she was a friend of mine, I always considered her like my sister, and my mother gave her a name, "*Uwacu,*" meaning, "one of us." We fixed an appointment on when and where to meet.

I then met all three of them in one of the well-known Internet cafés. Smiling, Marion said, "Are you Costa?" and I said I was. She was reflecting a wisdom and peace. I planned to take them to a ceremony for the ending of a one-week mourning period of my brother's father-in-law who had passed away. We went there and visited the Nyamata Genocide memorial site prior to the commencement of the ceremony. My American guests could not imagine how relatives killed their relatives, how almost one million innocent people were killed within a hundred days.

37

On the bus on the way back from Nyamata to Kigali, Marion and her husband Keith wanted to know much more about me, and my family. And some of the questions were: *"Were you here during the Genocide?" "Was your wife here?" "What do you do?"* As I have never had someone asking me such questions. I felt credibility and started narrating to them my background. At moments as I answered, my heart was grief-stricken and sometimes I held my breath to avoid crying on the bus and I felt ashamed to say a lot to the guests. Keith and his family left Rwanda with my e-mail address and they left me their business card. They run their businesses in Panama.

Since then this family has been very close to us. I will not forget one moment: my wife was chased out from an exam because she was irregular with paying school fees. She started crying and thinking about how other fortunate students were regular with payments because of their parents, or their husbands. At that moment, I again felt useless to my wife. When, hopelessly, she thought she would not be able to finish her academic year, we were surprised when Marion, Keith, and Genevieve sent one thousand dollars, which covered two academic years. That timely kindness touched our hearts deeply.

Marion is familiar with "The Work of Byron Katie" and when she and her husband went back to the United States they contacted Byron Katie International, suggesting that I and four other Rwandans should attend The School for The Work with Byron Katie.

In my wife's mail box, I first received Byron Katie's CDs and books and shared them with my friends who were preparing to go to The School in Los Angeles. We were all riveted by her book, *Loving What Is.* However, I was reading it as if it were a legend. When I was reading this book, gradually my mind was telling me that I suffered a lot but could not notice that.

That was Katie's little business, I repeatedly said that. It occurred to me to consider that the difficult situations I had gone through, and that I was going through, were the worst in the world. That is true, since I am the one who hosted the grieving and not someone else. Suffering is personal and there is no way I can compare my suffering to other people's suffering. The way each and every person is broken-hearted is quite unique.

I and other four Rwandans were very lucky to receive scholarships and even donated airfare tickets. The School was at the Marriot Hotel, Los Angeles. Many Africans like me know Los Angeles because of moviemakers, and superstars like the late Michael Jackson, Rambo, Schwarzenegger, Beverly Hills . . . .

Somehow, The Work is there, to bring peace in many homes, peace in many societies, peace in individuals, which was much more my new vital discovery area of life.

Ecstatically being for the first time on a plane, British Airways, I happily gave thanks to Byron Katie International for having enabled me to travel in the "Air." I was openly telling this to my Rwandan fellows on board. Heathrow Airport London was the first connection where I was totally disappointed and found difficulties walking on the escalators.

Our second connection was at JFK Airport, New York. I was very tired and hungry. Food was expensive and the only option was to wait uncomplainingly for when I would again be on board from JFK Airport to Los Angeles, which my hunger timing did not match. I found out in the air that there was no food provision on local flights.

Arriving at Los Angeles Airport, October 18, 2008, I and my Rwandan fellows were warmly welcomed by Marion, Keith, their daughter Genevieve and friends. We were hosted in a gigantic and fabulous building in Beverly Hills. That time I could not hold my tears. I was shown to my room and I told them that I wanted to have a nap. I could not ask for food since I was sad to see what that city looked like. My mind formed many questions and all of them were based on the imbalance between Beverly Hills and my country. Some of the questions were, "*What did these people give to God in order to get all these fabulous buildings?*" "*How is a child who was born in this city going to grow up?*" I could not imagine how this shocking imbalance came between people, and tears were falling out from my eyes.

I remember what happened to me and to my family when I was young. We were frequently upset to see our Congolese neighbors cooking, while all of us gathered around our mother without even hope to eat tomorrow. Tearful, my mother said to us that we had to understand the life of exile and she added that we were fatherless, so starving was something normal to us.

Whose business is it when I grieve because of what my mind gathered and echoed in me? Children have to grow up in Beverly Hills because they have to. I grew up in Democratic Republic of Congo because I had to grow up there. However, my mind kept reminding me that my life had been spoiled by the worst situations I had experienced for years and years before.

We had to spend seven days before we went to the school. It was another "unfortunate" opportunity for my mind to show me "I was useless for this World." Why that? The answer in my mind was that "only nice, bright people are here in Los Angeles." The proof was what my mind was showing to me daily! I could hear whispers in my ears, "*Look at that Villa! Look at this magic huge building!*" We got the chance to be taken to some wonderful places and events in Los Angeles.

Jill, the owner of the house we were staying in, and her husband John, took me to a church service one morning. That was at Agape International Spiritual Center. I had never been in such a huge church before. The inside was miraculously shining and my mind flew me to our church *Horebu Pentecostal* where 2,500 Christians gather in a room 30 meters square with frequent electricity lapses and few lamps. After the church service, we went to a massive AIDS Walk where it seemed we were the only Africans there, with our American friend allied.

Next was Disneyland, which was totally stunning and a fear challenger. We went then to Hollywood where I saw celebrity star tags on the ground across sidewalks. I saw those whom most African children favored. I remember several times as a kid I sweated in child labor in order to get money that would enable me to enter the movie centers to see Jackie Chan, Schwarzenegger, and Rambo. I sorrowfully told this to my American friends and said my brother Leopold could witness this too. I felt so sad to notice that those movie stars did not recognize that there are many African children who are engaged in the worst child labor to get money in order to see their movies.

One night before we went to The School for The Work, Marion's husband Keith, carefully told us that we would not be allowed to receive or to make calls during the School. He surprisingly bought for us phone call units through the Internet. I wanted to be the first to call home and tell them how poor, miserable, and unfortunate Africans are. I called my wife Bernadette and when she picked up the phone, without greetings I sorrowfully said, "We are walking but already dead."

She said, "Why?"

I replied, "Have you ever heard of a country where mosquito netting is useless?" It was too hard to make her understand that for a full seven days I did not see a mosquito or a fly. Moreover, I told her that I saw people eating whenever they wanted to! That was unbelievable to a person like me who rarely ate twice a day especially where I grew up in Uvira, Democratic Republic of Congo.

That night I did a presentation in Jill's house in Beverly Hills. Everyone was curious to hear what happened and what is happening now to most Africans and Rwandans. I knew much more about myself, my home country and countries where I lived before; but not all of Africa. It was very difficult for me to say things about myself. I was very ashamed and enchained by my stressful thoughts. Apart from my brother Leopold, no one among the Rwandans who were with us in Beverly Hills knew that I had been in prison three times.

> *When people take a fearful and rigid stance they*
> *often bring about what they are trying to prevent.* —
> Byron Katie, from *I Need Your Love—Is It True?*

# CHAPTER 5

# Nine Days with Byron Katie

I embarked to The School for The Work at Marriot Hotel close to the Los Angeles Airport known as LAX and was totally disappointed. I did not know what The School was going to realistically be like. However, from the CDs I listened to and the books I read by Byron Katie, I could picture what The School intended to be like.

The hotel was comprised of different movements of people walking up stairs, others down; some sliding escalators up, others down; three to five people or more riding the elevator, calmly looking in his or her own direction. It was a very giddy opportunity for me to use escalators since they are rare in my country.

Something brand new for me was that after check-in I was given a card, and it was called a key, which took my mind a long time to understand and use properly.

I was assigned as roommate to a Jewish man. We did not introduce ourselves to each other until the following day. I like interaction, much like many Africans, but what I observed that day was everyone quietly moving. I needed to follow their examples and behavior. Some people were very inquisitive and murmured, "Where are you from?" I replied "Rwanda" and got from them: "Oooh!"

The only place you could hear some multiple voices was in the registration room. Many activities were going on there including ticking one's presence, getting a name tag, taking ID photographs and gathering School material.

As designed, the night introduction started with a meditation. I was not used to meditation. Where I grew up, many people were not accustomed to meditation. I remember in childhood we were told meditation was the way that Marabous communicated with the devils.

The most fearful moment I met during that introductive part of The Work was meditation! During this process I was experiencing a mind battle within me. It was a good time to focus on the ways that could bring peace. My mind was engaged in the field of competition to know, which, between the stress and peace, will remain with me?

That first meditation for me was unsuccessful. I was preoccupied with seeing how many people were calmly seated. The silence was absolute with the exception of a cough here or there. During meditation, all the lights were off which was supposed to help us tap into our own insight. Soon the meditation ended with Byron Katie's words breaking the silence, "How was it?" and at the same time the lights flicked on. Instantly my skin was covered by goose bumps.

What happened? I saw Byron Katie seated in a large gray simple chair on the little stage, providing a slightly peaceful smile to the participants. That smile made me remember my wedding, when I and my wife went to hug my mother. It was the smile of a lovely mother before her lovely children.

I recognized the face I had seen several times on the website, books, and CD covers. There she was—Byron Katie—with a clear, direct voice. She was framed by two peaceful nature scenes. On a small table there was a purple cup of tea and a gorgeous vase of flowers. She was serious but could also laugh and smile at the same time. She could spontaneously stop her smile. She could enthusiastically respond to every question and seemed indifferent to the impact of her answers.

A friend of mine revealed to me that he liked The School for The Work but failed to complete it. Inquisitively I asked him why he failed. He told me that he feared to publicly state his concerns. "I have never raised my hand," he told me. "I feared to face Byron Katie. Her questions seem to be like spears to my mind." "**I**" **believed that!**

Next all participants had to introduce themselves by simply saying their name and where they came from. We were then given the agenda for the following day, which would start with a very interesting morning walk. I knew one thing, "Every activity is going to be done in silence." Hearing was the most important part. Around 10 pm we all went in our rooms. I met my brother Leopold and asked him how the first night was. He said, "Let's wait and see what The School will mean to us." He asked me, "How was it to you?" I told him that I had a hard time meditating. When I closed my eyes in such a silent atmosphere, I felt confusion within. It was awful to meditate. Again I told him that I could not understand how the schedule for one day could start at 7:30 am and go up to 10 pm. My mind was apprehensively bringing confusion.

The following day, no sooner had I woken up than I was quickly on the Walk which was preceded by a gathering of all participants where I could hear a megaphoned instruction speech saying, "Walk in silence…"

My heart was beating to experience this very first concentrated, meditative walk.

When the walk was done, I came to realize that it was connecting me with nature and I started seeing how much the universe is lovely.

After a fabulous breakfast we went to the room and started with the prompted morning meditation. Every morning, School was preceded by a meditation, which intermittently ended with Byron Katie's soft, soothing, "Good morning." Then voluntarily, the participants started to present their reactions to the meditation, dreams, everything. Most of Byron Katie's reactions were confusing me. She often would simply say, "Thank you."

On that second day, Byron Katie helped me to bring my mind in the field of The Work by letting me and my classmates know about the process of The Work, which I read and re-read in Rwanda and could not understand its effectiveness. However, I did realize that The Work of Byron Katie, which I considered to be a minor path to stopping my longtime pain, concerned the four questions and the Turnaround.

1. *Is it true?*
2. *Can you absolutely know that it's true?*
3. *How do you react, what happens, when you believe that thought?*
4. *Who would you be without the thought?*

   *Then turn around the concept you are questioning, and don't forget to find at least three genuine, specific examples of each turnaround.* (See www. thework.com)

The process was just an invitation. I needed to identify my stressful thoughts about any past situation that I had experienced, present experiences, and possible future experiences. The process was to write down and start questioning my mind using a *Yellow Card* bearing the Four Questions. I was given a paper called the Judge Your Neighbor Work Sheet (see www.thework. com) that could guide me to record my stressful thoughts.

I was in a real battle and was confused. Which stressful thought should I put on paper? I had many things inside myself. My life was characterized by very bad experiences. I should start with the fact of seeing myself in a room with white people and remembering my mother saying, "White people were the ones who brought the Genocide of thousands and thousands of Tutsis in 1959, which resulted in our unfortunate life of exile." She was telling me that all the hatred that was spread throughout Rwandan communities was started by white people. My Aunt Anastasie would tell us about the Roman Catholic Bishop André Perraudin who successfully educated and supported the so-called Rwandans in hating their relatives.

I grew up hating white people, and I was wondering if I could start with that.

Then I wondered if I should rather start with my three unforgettable detentions in the worst, grimy, small prisons in the Democratic Republic of Congo, in Burundi, after being seriously and miserably tortured, and in Rwanda. Then came the thought about the guy who killed my wife's mother in a very brutal, heartless way during the Rwandan Tutsis' Genocide. Or was it important to put on paper, first, my stressful thoughts I had of those who killed my uncles, cousins, and my wife's father and siblings?

There was a sudden surging flow of bad memories and I made a decision to not put anything on the paper.

I told my partner I was not ready.

Everyone who experienced The School for The Work with Byron Katie was kind. I remember when I was telling some of the staff that I was not ready, they were replying with a very soft and peaceful "*Okay.*"

After the exercise of questioning the stressful thoughts using both the Judge Your Neighbor Work Sheet and the Yellow Card with Four Questions, participants came together in the room and those who could willingly share their experience were allowed to do so.

I noticed that people who were sharing intensely read their statements containing the stressful thoughts on what they had experienced or were experiencing, and they always ended up smiling. That was not really my business.

My understanding up to the third day was that I was grieving and hurting in a way that no one else had ever experienced. One of the main actions chosen by my mind was to keep quiet and not tell this to everybody.

Many people think this way. Not telling what frustrates me is one way of having peace, yet inside I was full of confusion and conflict. I had been experiencing this for a long time before I did my inquiry. My lovely wife, a Genocide survivor, was also one of the people who decided to keep quiet pretending to be living in peace, yet she was a victim of trauma crisis, especially during the period of remembering the Tutsis' Genocide every April to July.

That third day of The School was very challenging for me. I was very sad and hating deeply The Work, which I considered a process that was taking me back to my sufferings and wrongly making me revive them. As proof of that, my mind was telling me to look around at how people were screaming while sharing their life experiences after being facilitated to do the inquiry. However, I did also notice that always after their tears, they ended with smiles.

I was still resisting writing my stressful thoughts on the Judge Your Neighbor Work Sheet and found the peaceful solution was to keep quiet. On that same day before we went to dinner, I met my brother Leopold and asked him how he was experiencing The Work. He told me, "I do understand the process. The four questions are very powerful and I was wondering how you are going to respond. I did not have as many sufferings as you had in my life and it is going to be painful for you to answer and question your mind." He added, "I tried but I failed to *turn around* my statement, since it is a very difficult part to bear responsibility for the one who hurt you."

I was advised by my mind to dodge the last part of that third day and went in my room. One of the staff called directly to the room and told me to do my best to come. He was very kind when talking, "Costa if you are tired, can you come to rest here in the class room and if you want, you can bring your pillow." I did just that to respect his instruction.

That night after the last session of the third day, I went to meet Marion, who had connected me with The Work of Byron Katie, and told her that I was not on the right track and instead of getting peace in me, I was getting sufferings instead. I told her that The Work was taking me back to all the worst situations I came across during my life. I could not write down my stressful thoughts, which just seemed to revive them again. Marion advised me, "If you failed to write down what is making you suffer it is okay; be strong tomorrow in the room, raise your hand and tell that to Byron Katie." Wow, my heart started beating. I got an alarm reminder from my mind of that friend who did not complete his inquiry because of fearing Byron Katie's questions. I fearfully decided to raise my hand and face Byron Katie's questions.

All night long I could not sleep and I was in deep confusion on how I was going "*to live again*" my sorrowful experiences. I thought I was not living peacefully; instead I still hated many people who hurt me. We always think of being peaceful, yet our heart is full of grievances and hatred. That was the status of my life whereby I was always thinking that I should not say something regarding the people, areas, and stories that were connected with my terrible experiences. I was really supporting the idea of my wife who was always telling me to just keep quiet and not talk about what hurt me.

In the morning of my fourth day when I was in the Morning Walk, one of my favorite parts of The School for The Work with Byron Katie, I was in deep confusion and wondering about my commitment to raise my hand in the room and say publicly one of my stressful stories. Normally after the morning walk all participants go directly for breakfast, which I dodged that day. My heart was beating and felt full of fear and anger. But the commitment was there.

That morning! That morning! That morning I will not forget in my life, when my mind was in a great contest with me, the day of ending my sufferings and discovering the way of the truth.

We entered the room and started the morning meditation, which again was difficult for me since it was characterized by a strong inner struggle. I started consciously realizing that all the suffering I had experienced was inside me, and my mind mistakenly was lying to me that the only way to find peace was to keep quiet and not talk about my stressful thoughts.

After the meditation, my hand was very weighty when I tried to raise it and there was an inner voice insisting, *"Stop revealing your sufferings in this room."* I started crying and panicking. I believed what my mind told me and that morning, I did not raise my hand. Despite my earlier commitment to break silence, I did not raise my hand.

The reason that came to my mind was: *If I said one of my experiences in my life, I could be torturing myself by reviving the hurtful moment. I could cry publicly and then my brother Leopold could condemn me and the other three Rwandans who were in The School and who never knew about my unfortunate life experiences, would then be aware of them. Another problem, which was much more serious and awful, was to face the four questions and terribly be questioned by Byron Katie.*

However, there was another voice in me, which was telling me how talking about my stressful experience might be the right way to *download* my heart. I felt so weak to not meet my commitment.

During lunchtime I decided to go to my room, since the battle was continuing inside me, and found my roommate, who asked me, "How are you doing Costa?"

I barely replied to him that I was doing well. He said, "Let's go for lunch," and I said that I would come later.

I remained in the room and started thinking about how to make my decision of presenting my hurtful statement in the room at 2 pm after lunch break.

> *"Your first job, therefore, is to remember your magnificence, and your second job is to stand firm in your own greatness."* —Dr. Jim Lockard, *Sacred Thinking*

Two pm. We all gathered and started the meditation. Even before Byron Katie's custom of ending the meditation process by asking, "*How was it?*" My hand was up! I couldn't hide myself any longer. Even as I wrote this very paragraph, my heart was beating as my mind remembered that powerful unforgottable moment.

I was the first to put my hand up and instantly other hands were up. Mine could be seen easily since it was the only one of dark chocolate color. "*Costaaaa!*" Byron Katie surprisingly called me and told me to come toward her.

I was sitting in the back row. From my seat to the front of the room was a very long and hard journey though the diameter of the room was approximately 40 meters, 131 footsteps. She stood up and came to meet me. She was smiling but my face was fearful and my mind in total confusion. The impending result was unknown. The way I saw Byron Katie walking toward me was totally unusual. I always saw her walking very fast, but now she walked meditatively, looking straight into my eyes. I felt as if I were mad-crazy at that time. My mind was notifying me that Katie was hunting me. I felt as if I was being attacked and I was powerless.

I remember my hurtful statement I came up with derived from Seromba, the guy who killed my wife's mother during the Tutsis' Genocide. He slaughtered her and cut off her breasts before throwing her body in a hole and covering it with a bunch of stones. All this was done when my wife Bernadette, seventeen years old at the time, was with her brother Yves, watching, through fans in a ceiling of a house where they hid. That ruthless act was committed when mother's last born daughter, Denise, was almost two years old, and was crying out to be breastfed. She could not know what was happening to her mother.

I therefore came up with my statement, "*I am frustrated with Seromba because he slaughtered my mother-in-law.*" I could not say her name though she had passed away. In most African countries you honor your mother-in-law so highly that you can't say her name publicly. I grew up with and lived with such belief.

Katie went on with the Questions:

1. Byron Katie: *Seromba slaughtered your mother-in-law, Is that true?*
   "I": *My mind was very critical and started seeing Katie like a sadist who purposefully wanted to break my heart. After a few minutes of sweating I said, "Yes!"*

2. Byron Katie: *Seromba slaughtered your mother-in-law; Can you absolutely know that it's true?*
   "I": *Shaking my head at the same time I said, "Yes!" I was shivering, shaking, sweating, and my heart was pounding loudly. Byron Katie's eyes were seriously fixed on my eyes.*

3. Byron Katie: *How do you react, what happens, when you believe that thought, Seromba slaughtered your mother-in-law?*
   "I": *I started to stammer, a characteristic that was totally new to me. I responded I was always wishing Seromba would kill himself and leave this World. My reaction was really about revenge.*

4. Byron Katie: *Who would you be without the thought, Seromba slaughtered your mother-in-law?*
"I": *With a very deep breath, my answer was of course peaceful, I replied, "I would live peacefully and lovely."*

Then Byron Katie went on to the part of the *Turnaround.*

Byron Katie: *Costa, Seromba slaughtered your mother-in-law, can you turn it around? And then give one —*
I got a deep breath. Closing my eyes and said, "I can't turn around!"

Byron Katie told me, "Costa, believe me and just try to turn around your statement, *"Seromba slaughtered your mother-in-law."*
I replied saying," No, I can't!"

Byron Katie again said, *"Seromba did that once in 1994; by the time that you are bringing that idea back, and back, and back, and back, you have that image on how Seromba got a machete and slaughtered your mother-in-law. You have that in your mind and you are the one who is killing her in your mind today. Seromba today is peaceful and you, you are suffering!"*

I fell into tears and slowly, moving inside me, found a deep psychological understanding of what Byron Katie was speaking. I clandestinely turned around in my heart and found I was slaughtering my mother-in-law in my mind at any time I thought about what Seromba did, and felt anger, hatred, and full of inner conflict.

There was a reality that started sounding in me. I went on with the thought *"Seromba today is peaceful and you, you are suffering!"*

I instantly fell into Byron Katie hands and hugged her. I could feel her hug tenaciously telling me, *"You have to make your peace and live lovely."*

That night of the fourth day after my hard inquiry facilitated by Byron Katie, I was feeling like someone returned from battle, and positively. Despite the fact that I was really hungry, I could not go in the dining room; I was rather thinking much more about how I was feeling.

While I was meditating in my room, suddenly I had a mind alarm and the curtain was open and I started seeing the reality that was missing in my life.

Ah! I had decided to start the inquiry afresh by going from the first question up to the fourth.

*Is it true?*

This question took me from a starting point of my inquiry and moved me across the process.

*Can you absolutely know that it's true?*

I stopped there and started wondering what the fundamental importance of asking myself that question was. It helped me analyze if my stressful thought had an essential reason to stay in me. Again, it helped me go deep and bring that stressful thought to the reality of "The Present" where I was in the room of a hotel in Los Angeles, and imagining what happened to my mother-in-law.

*How do you react, what happens, when you believe that thought?*

There I was in the center of my inquiry. It was like someone who was going to commit suicide and he got "a chance" to be asked, "*If you are going to commit suicide, who is going to suffer? The one who hurt you or, are you the one who is going to lose your life?*"

That third question "*How do you react, what happens, when you believe that thought?*" broadened my inquiry that night and assisted me to go deep and discover different results in my inner conflict.

Wow, then came again another inquiry when facing that third question, "Whose business is it when I am angry, upset, frustrated, full of conflict, and when I am grieving?"

Oh! I was really in pain, full of sorrow and inner turbulence when I accepted to "*accommodate and live with my stressful story.*"

On that step of the third question, I was identifying all the results of my profound sorrow.

I noticed that since I was connected and "utilized" my nerve-racking story, I could not contemplate love and peace. Rather my mind was preoccupied with revenge.

I remember one day my wife was telling me about one of the guys involved in the murder of her relatives and I said, "He should be killed."

Several times, I myself attempted to go to Congo to find Sergeant Pongo, who was demobilized after the former Democratic Republic of Congo army lost power, or, instead, find his children and do something bad to them as paying him back for having arrested me arbitrarily and throwing me into such terrible conditions. During all that period, Pongo was living nonviolently, while I was the one obsessed with violence.

When I live with my stressful story, I react pitilessly; sometimes I will even discriminate against people I interact with.

That third question revealed to me that I was bearing all the sufferings and then generating a "*so-called peace system*" such that I was not talking much about my life experience, instead thinking rather on revenge and all kinds of aggressive imaginings.

It was much harder to discover what reaction my way of living with conflict was creating in me. I started noticing how many times I fell sick when I was thinking about how I failed to track down Pongo or his children to take revenge for my detention and tortures. I felt happy when I heard about the death of the Burundian policeman who arrested me and had beaten me almost to death. Many times I went through a crisis, as I returned to all of those stories, spending days without talking to my child or to orphans who were living with me. Again, my mind was focusing on such things as how on several occasions my wife would not eat or even go to work when she was reminded of her family being killed during the Genocide.

Then I went on with my inquiry by confronting myself, "What was really my benefit out of that Burundian policeman's death?" When we are stressful we sometimes think that we can get peace when someone dies.

Moving on to that third question of the inquiry "*How do you react, what happens, when you believe that thought?*" that night I came up with the idea noticing that it was time to question my mind on different reactions resulting from the fact of being angry, frustrated, isolated, conflicted, depressed, and hateful.

The matter was, "What have I been getting out of my detestable situation, which I was living with?" **Peace or Hatred?** This current working situation was a timely opportunity to take my time to balance and discover the genuine truth.

I liked my mind at that time: on the one hand it could alarm me with fear; thankfully, on the other hand, it could also alert me easily with peace. Peace was there and I was trying hard to pull it out from where it was hiding in me.

*Who would you be without the thought?*

After asking myself this question, I breathed deeply. It was a nice step toward feeling peace.

I started noticing that stress and worry within me were releasing and it improved my primary relationships by increasing my clear communication and understanding.

I began to stop worrying about other people whom I have no control over.

I began to stop whipping myself up for being weak and this reduces my stress levels considerably. I now know that my stressful thoughts were simply torturing my life.

Fundamentally, I will not forget my stressful thoughts, but I must not seize them. Not using my stressful thoughts includes the revengeful spirit, hating objects, names, tribes, areas, and people who were in connection with what happened to me during my detentions, since I did not have control over them.

Without those thoughts I could be living lovely. I imagined, how, before my stories, what kind of life I was experiencing. I did not know anything about prison, anything about torture, anything about suffering, meaning that I was living peacefully.

Therefore, if I was choosing to live in my past stories, could I not, did I not, have the potential to also bring beautiful moments and live with them?

My past was about both pain and happiness. What I was choosing to live with was what I was experiencing.

During my interaction with that question "*Who would you be without the thought?*" I discovered a more peaceful space and noticed that my time was "that moment," and not in the past, not even in the future. I was seeing my life through a different lens.

I was like someone who wanted to open the door and could not easily find the key. After looking for it here and there, suddenly I found the key in my pocket. Oh! My God, that could be said by many North Americans after finding an object in a place they could not believe to be there. I was convinced that my peace was recovered and could not miss that chance.

I held there and continued to interact with my mind by showing it how fear was the foundation of my suffering. It was very difficult for me to live "The Present" when my mind was always reminding me how much I was defeated in my life and I could take revenge, or opt to keep quiet.

As a Christian, I knew that God did not bring me in this World only to suffer. Several times, we were taught that God wants us to always be happy.

He does not Himself rely on our stories since He always said, "Just knock and I will open." He lives "The Present," ready to forgive our sins at any given time.

Why should I not live "The Present" and live peacefully? I could have control of all those people I was blaming to have hurt me.

A perfect realization was when I knew that the good and peaceful reality would not come from outside, rather from inside me, after of course doing The Work and finding out where it is hidden.

Come with me from the first question of the inquiry up to the fourth question, "*Who would you be without the thought?*" I was realizing the power of the inquiry of The Work, which was channeling me toward a peaceful way.

Consciously, I knew that my mind was not my enemy; rather The Work reminded me that my mind can engage my life in a battle; ultimately, it can also engage me in a lovely and peaceful life.

My mind could then understand that fear was at the center of my grievance. Why should I stay angry at what hideously happened when I did not have a choice? Every spiteful action that happened to me happened because it had to happen and I did not have any choice before in those circumstances.

During the same night in my room, I looked at my body, which has scars from the physical persecutions by Congolese (former Zaïrian) soldiers, who walloped me with knives attached to the guns, burnt me with their cigarettes, kicked me with their boots, and found that "The Present" told me to see those scars as scars—not as injuries.

The reality was that they were only scars, no longer painful injuries. They looked as colored spots on my skin and not wounds. I could not see them again as injuries as I was seeing them before questioning my mind. I dropped that illusory way of thinking and knew the veracity within me. The reality was revealed.

The light of my life was inside me and was almost covered by fear, which was there at the center of all my suffering.

It was so inspiring to me to notice that it was impossible for me to return my age back up to seventeen and be again in the Congolese cell or in the Burundian prison, or even take my age back from now to the year 2000 when I was detained in my country's jail or to any period I was experiencing tortures, hunger, and a sorrowful life of exile with my unfortunate widow mom. I do not have any power to control my past and even to live it, I told this to that part of my mind, which always imports stressful stories and wants me to live them and even use them in my everyday life.

Wow, it is unworkable to rewind the day cycle of a calendar and change this to the way I want. My mind was open and started realizing the truth. I can even rejoice that my past is past and not continue to live it.

I knew that things were the way I knew them inside me and that the entire scenario was produced and reproduced by my fearful mind.

It was then time for me to move forward with the Turn-around part of the inquiry, which was always difficult for me even when I was practicing The Work in Rwanda and when I was facilitated by Byron Katie.

But I said, "Let's try." I went in to space and got a deep breath and read the statement, I did that same day, "*Seromba slaughtered your mother-in-law.*" I knew how to say this but I was again stuck. I felt the statement to be much heavier and could not simply turn it around.

Normally, the Turnaround is always followed by some genuine examples related to your Turnaround statement.

I went on with some simple sentences, trying to turn them around and found genuine examples.

The Question was asked and answered by myself.

*God did not care when I was tortured by Burundian police and Congolese soldiers at a teen age.*

God does not care. *Is that true?*

Yes!

God does not care. *Can you absolutely know that it's true?*

Inside me came the image of seeing myself without clothes, naked, pushed down in mud, beaten by Congolese soldiers using car brake wire cables, and I said, "Yes!"

God does not care. *How do you react, what happens, when you believe that thought?*

I felt God to be partially and even fully unsympathetic to me. I was suffering; at any time I have the thought and remember the way I was screaming, "*Mungu! Mungu! Mungu!*" meaning, "God! God! God!" My screaming was in vain. It happened to the point where I did not want to go to church when I had that thought and felt weak.

God does not care. *Who would you be without that thought?* I would be peaceful and faithful to God.

God does not care. *Turn around the statement and give more than three examples.*

God cares!

First example: I knew some guys who were beaten in the same Congolese jail and afterwards died from shock and injuries. Praise God I survived.

Second example: I remembered, how, when we were in exile in the Democratic Republic of Congo, many children were dying from kwashiorkor, a state of malnutrition I also suffered but did not die from.

Third example: I knew many teenagers who were arbitrarily arrested and put in that Burundian jail where I was detained and they spent even more than a year and, after, they were transferred to the main prison where they endured years and years without any trials. I was not there that long and I said, "*It was by God's sake.*"

A fourth example: I am alive.

Next: God does not care, another *Turn around the statement and give more than three examples.*

I don't care!

First example: I remember several times when I thought on what happened to me and I could not eat or hardly sleep.

Second example: Thinking about revenge was also another fact of not taking care of my personality. On the other way, I was devaluating my personality as a human by choosing the way of being malevolent.

Third example: By hating others, I hate myself; I do not have peace in me.

God does not care, another *Turn around the statement and give more than three examples:*

My mind told me that, "God does not."

First example: No one told me that God does not care, just my mind told me that and I did believe.

Second example: When my mind is fearful it always tells me that blame goes to God. It told me that God is indifferent.

Third example: I agreed with everything my mind was telling me.

Back to my first statement, "*Seromba slaughtered your mother-in-law.*" I was again and again stuck and I did understand it was really difficult for me to turn around.

However, I felt peace inside me and started thinking about how I could do more and more inquiries on all issues that were "unfairly torturing my mind" and making me believe I was trapped in that status irretrievably.

I was very hungry; my roommate was not in the room and around 11:00 pm one of my Rwandan friends who was in the training brought me an apple and found me in a good mood that she was surprised to meet me in. I was smiling and told her,

"Thank you." She asked me if I was doing well and I replied that I was going very well and added that I progressively found truth discovery behind The Work.

The Work of Byron Katie became for me a way of finding freedom and inner peace. I realized that my sufferings grew from my mind when the latter became fearful and now knew how to interact with it from a true inner peace.

I had consistently experienced how I was torturing my life by living with conflict, which I could not share with anyone.

The five remaining days for The School for The Work, helped me enjoy the other World of understanding. However, I had some additional stories to inquire on. Yes! "That was just the beginning," as Byron Katie used to say.

I was extremely curious to continue doing The Work at any relaxed time and even invite my Rwandan fellows who were with me in The School to participate. I could easily approach my brother Leopold and invite him to do The Work.

He was flexible and so was I.

One day before we ended, we had a wonderful graduation ceremony. Everyone was called publicly by his name and presented with a diploma.

My turn had not yet come. I was thinking much more about the harvest I had reaped from the four days of turbulence and five days of peace. I confidently told my mind that, "The diploma I am going to get, is dedicated to you." The reason behind this was that my mind changed from fearfulness to flexibleness.

I was then called by my first name, Costa, which is simple to pronounce, and graduated into a way of living I still practice to this very day.

I mean, consider, what is more frightening than being in conflict? Several times when I felt being hated, being in conflict,

I could not be confident I was even doing things accurately. My fear was the source of insecurity and conflict.

Normally the last Work session was a quarter of a day and concluded at noon. No lunch provided. You need to buy one for yourself. Our friend Marion, her husband Keith, their Genevieve, and their Canadian friend Autumn, took us to a McDonald's restaurant. While we were waiting for our orders I found one guy who was discussing basketball issues. He said, "Basketball is an African-American game." He was saying this to the other two guys who were lifting up and down their heads showing that they were complying with his notice. My mind asked me, "Is that true?" I wanted to know about the reason why African-Americans are the only ones who play basketball.

I approached and introduced myself to them. "My name is Costa, I am from Africa." They asked me what country of Africa I came from. I said, "Rwanda."

Abruptly the same guy who was giving his observation on basketball said, "Wow, that is a country of murderers."

I said, "Rwanda is among the most peaceful countries in the world today."

I asked if I could share something with them. They replied positively and I handed them the yellow card containing the four questions of The Work process and said, "Can you please go on with these questions by asking yourself about the African-American basketball observation you were discussing?" One of them was very interested and asked me how they could do that.

I replied "Just go with that: 'Basketball is an African-American game,' then hand to your partner the yellow card and he can start asking you these questions on it":

1. *Is it true?*
2. *Can you absolutely know that it's true?*
3. *How do you react, what happens, when you believe that thought?*
4. *Who would you be without the thought?*

Then turn around that observation "basketball is an African-American game" and give some genuine examples.

Expressly, one of them stated that he knew many European basketball players who professionally play in the United States.

I felt happy with that and I said, "Please use those questions for any stressful thought that comes to you. I invited them to consider the statement earlier spoken about Rwanda. "Rwanda is a country of murderers." I rushed to my nice burger, which I knew I could hardly find in Rwanda.

I did not have more extended time to spend in Los Angeles as neither did my other Rwandan fellows. However, we were invited again to have a pizza, which in our country is known by few people. The wonderful person Jill Hilarion, who hosted us in Beverly Hills, and her friend Autumn Drouin, who were at the same time staffing The School for The Work, offered that precious meal. At the table sharing the food, I told my friends that I felt very surprised the same way I felt the days I was released from jail, especially the one in Congo.

We subsequently headed to the airport and were well accompanied with our heavy suitcases full of different gifts.

Two things happened at the Los Angeles airport and The Work was there to help us by showing the reality and creating calm.

The first problem was that my ticket showed two final destinations, Kigali airport which was my preferable destination since it is my home city, and Entebbe, Uganda, in another country and far from my home. The check-in officer looked at my E-ticket and said that there was some confusion. She went to ask her supervisor and my heart was beating in a wait-and-see manner. Soon she came shaking her head in a negative sense. She told me that she was sorry, there was a mistake during the E-ticket purchase, and "You will need to land to Entebbe, Uganda." However, she added saying that we could contact the office of the airline company from where we got from the ticket. That office was in O'Hare airport.

I was very fearful to be landing in Entebbe, Uganda at 11:00 pm with all my heavy suitcases. I did not have enough money to pay for an airfare ticket from Entebbe, Uganda to Kigali, Rwanda. The alternative was to take a taxi cab to Kampala, the Ugandan capital city, and spend one night there, and then gets the bus in the morning to Kigali, Rwanda. Meanwhile, I was confused and something funny was happening; my mind was already traveling in a stressful spirit which was giving me an image on how I was going to suffer. My brother Leopold and our American friends and our lovely Canadian friend Autumn, were focusing their minds on trying to see if they could get another alternative.

I clandestinely withdrew my steps backwards and considered the stress and anger which were building up inside of me. So the matter was, "Travelling through Entebbe is tiresome."

I went with that inquiry:
Traveling through Entebbe, Uganda is tiresome,

1. *Is it true?*
2. *Can I absolutely know that it's true?*
3. *How do I react when I have that thought "Travelling through Entebbe, Uganda is tiresome?"*

I was feeling very angry and talked badly to the lady who was at the check-in desk. I was treating myself in a careless manner by creating more and more suffering in me, which could not bring any solution at all.

Who would I be without the thought, "*Travelling through Entebbe, Uganda is tiresome?*" I would love being happier.

I went with a Turnaround, "*Travelling through Entebbe, Uganda isn't tiresome?*"

I did the same trip from Kigali, Rwanda to Los Angeles. Wow, I came to realize that again my fearful mind, which did not have any power to control the outside, was causing alarm in me.

As I was navigating through that world of confusion, my consciousness through fear and misinterpretation forced an obscure way of finding perception of reality. I touched my truth, I had to remind myself, to commit to—Self-finding through Self-inquiry. As I learned to absorb this experience of inquiry directly into my life, without constricting in fear or resistance, I began to feel peace. There came truth, the real truth that brought a bona fide understanding.

During that short and deep inquiry, Marion was struggling to help us take all the gifts we had so fortuitously received. She was courageously reducing the load of some suitcases by taking out some stuff and putting items in other suitcases with low loads. One person could not exceed two suitcases of 60 pounds each. She worked for an airline company before and easily knew how to handle that. She was trying to create balance for all suitcases. Sinuously, Marion managed to squeeze everything into six suitcases herself, zip them up and put them on the scale. Remarkably, all eight suitcases had 60 pounds each, only one small bag remained. That told me how peaceful and lovely Marion was.

My boarding pass was then printed showing that my final destination was Entebbe, Uganda. Being reinforced by the inquiry, I decided to "*Love what it is!*"

A voice came in me while boarding, "*If you think you are peaceful, get that statement inside you and feel and feel that.*" I knew how much we are bothered with something that we do not have control of. I remember my wife told me one day that "*Confusion is part of life.*" After the inquiry, I knew that, "*Everything is part of my life if I want it to be so.*"

Living with The Work became my way of controlling my spiritual part of life and changing the interactive process with my mind.

Our mind keeps actualizing the past and therefore we keep being outdated by experiencing all the stressful stories.

> *Without the stories, it's just not personal. You get to the place where you don't care whether you live or die, because you're having so much fun investigating these concepts.* —Byron Katie, *Question Your Thinking, Change the World*

Our first stop was O'Hare Airport in Chicago. We had eight hours of stopover there and my brother Leopold proposed an idea. *"Eight hours in the airport is too much; let us go to visit downtown Chicago."* I positively responded to that request since I knew once I visited that famous city, I could tell a lot to my friends and my family in Rwanda. We have heard about Chicago for a long time and some of our friends living in all the places I lived knew the Chicago Bulls, an eminent basketball team. We were committed to go there but we did not know how to get there.

I and my brother left the airport. It was *very easy to exit but hard to enter.* When we were outside we saw some trains doing come-and-go on an upper road. So we needed to find them since our minds told us that they were going to downtown Chicago. However to connect to these trains, we needed to walk. We were walking on the left side of the road very fast in order to minimize our time.

The road we were walking on contained many vehicles driving very fast and we had never seen cars with such speed. Some of the drivers put their hand outside their window and waved to us. Others were honking and waving at the same time. My brother thought that all those people were happy to see us, the only ones who were walking by foot. That was not the reality.

Soon a small police wagon came and parked backward to us. There came a policeman, who looked very short, and an advanced age, around sixty. He came toward us and I could see how furious he was. He shouted, "*Are you crazy? Are you crazy? Why are you walking on the freeway?*" We could not know what 'freeway' meant at that time. Loudly he recommended, "*Go over the wall.*" We went backward to the wall.

The following question was, "Where are you from?" We all responded, "Rwanda!"

My mind started vibrating and alarming that I was going to jail today. My heart was beating in an unusual way.

I was picturing my life in an American jail and getting my fourth jail life experience after those in Congo, Burundi, and Rwanda.

The policeman would not come close to us. He asked my brother, "How many feet are you?"

My brother Leopold could not understand that what he asked, I replied on his behalf, "We don't use feet for measurement."

He went on with another question, "How many pounds are you?"

I said, "We don't use pounds in our county; rather we use kilograms." I was shaking so much.

He told us to present our passports. Mine was in the inside pocket of my jacket. When I put my hand into my jacket to take it out, the abrupt fellow ran away fast and hid behind his car. Leopold whispered, "He thought you wanted to pull out a gun." He added, "We are in troubles." My mind sagged.

The officer called on his radio and within a very short period of time, there came four other police cars. One was full of dogs that were insistently barking. You can imagine the horror and terror filling our minds.

We were surrounded by eight policemen. After their short clandestine talk, one tall fellow approached closer. He was not as furious as the previous official, though he looked to be serious.

The first words he asked us were, "Why are you walking on the freeway?" I replied saying that we did not know what a freeway was.

He asked us where we were from. I replied, "From Rwanda."

He said, "You killed many people there."

This comment raised a very good aspect of The Work I was exercising. I heard a voice in my mind prompt "There, I am going to challenge you!" Producing a very self-assured smile, I offered "You are so outdated; that was in 1994 but now Rwanda is much more about love. Our country Rwanda is among the most peaceful ones in the world." He told us that many Americans still have in their minds the picture of Genocide in Rwanda.

He requested our passports. I was then careful and told him that my passport was in my jacket. For a short time he went in his car and after came and said, "Take it out."

He wanted to know the purpose of our trip to the United States and I spoke of the inquiry. He was so gentle and willing to hear. I told him that we came to the United States to attend School for The Work with Byron Katie in Los Angeles. I went further and let him know that the School was about helping people to know the truth.

"We also want to know the truth about why you are walking on the freeway?" he said, smilingly.

I told him that, seeing a Rwandan with a Genocidal picture today was not the truth and that resulted in suffering and fear. I added that, "You can't go to Rwanda today since you have in your mind *you killed many people.* So to know the truth you need to question your mind. For such a purpose we came to School for The Work."

I could see in him some peace arising and felt it coming in me as well. He asked us what our roads in Rwanda looked like. I told him that "they are narrow, and we don't have roads made exclusively for cars. Always you will find paths for pedestrians."

We were put in the police wagon. We used to see that kind of vehicle in movies, called a *paddy wagon,* used to carry people who committed crimes. Seated face-to-face, I and my brother, had a picture of being back in jail. "Anyway," I told Leopold, "I hope that American jails are not like African ones! Let us believe that we will not suffer there, or face torture."

A mind is very creative especially when it is full of fear. It sometimes projects our life even beyond reality and we then may believe nothing else but suffering.

That reminded me how often people cancel travel or commitments because of believing too much in their minds.

Questioning your mind can be a guiding way to get out from those kinds of confusions and finding the truth. I found that it is very requisite to ask my mind in any circumstance "Is it true?" then go with the inquiry.

We were much troubled in our own minds being in that police wagon since the police didn't tell us where we were going. Oh! That was not our business to put them under our control. I was confusingly laughing. After we were put in the police wagon, the police got some time to talk and spent more minutes before leaving that place. We couldn't know what they were talking about, but our minds were *"planning for them."* Why? Fear! They were still holding our passports and of course that was one of the bridges that my mind was using to amplify the situation. Inside me my mind insisted, *"You are going to jail for your fourth time."*

The Work intervened there. I asked my brother Leopold, "What is the matter which is causing us to sweat like this?"

He said, "We are going to suffer."

I told him; let's practice the inquiry on this. "We are going to suffer."

I told him to be a facilitator and I would act as a client.

Four questions to consider.

Costa: I am going to suffer.

Leopold: Is it true?

Costa: Yes!

Leopold: Can you absolutely know that it's true, you are going to suffer?

Costa: No!

Leopold: How do you react, what happens, when you believe that thought, you are going to suffer?

Costa: I am sweating, I feel so useless in this world. I am weak and hate everyone. I treat myself like a cursed person.

Leopold: Who would you be without the thought, you are going to suffer?

Costa: There I took an abrupt deep breath. I would accept this situation because I did not have control of it; rather I could control what is going on inside me. I would be peaceful.

The police wagon started moving. Its movement matched with the answer I was giving to the fourth question of the inquiry.

I requested Leopold finish with the Turnaround.

Leopold: You are going to suffer; can you turn that around and give some genuine examples?

Costa: I am not going to suffer!

Oh my God! The reality was that, nothing bad was done to me. I wasn't tortured; I wasn't insulted, even my brother Leopold experienced no bad action from the police. The police wagon was a much better vehicle compared to the ones we were used to in Congo when we travelled.

Wow! The police wagon stopped. Immediately we heard someone inserting the key in the door. A different policeman spoke. "Come out." The first thing we saw after being out was the entry doors of the airport.

We all stared. The policeman told us, "I liked the way you responded when one of us asked you guys about the mass-killings that happened in your country Rwanda." I personally suffer the same when my wife raises the issue of going to Rwanda for a visit. I noticed that we are much more attached to the story and our thoughts even overcome *The Present*. "You really touched my heart," he said. "I would like to continue talking with you, but I need to go." He asked us if we had a contact card. Of course! I gave him mine. He advised us to never walk again on the freeway. He pointed to a sign that restricts pedestrians, bikes, horses to enter the freeway.

I looked around to see if there were any horses.

When we were saying "Bye!" to him, my brother Leopold again came with the original concern, "We want to go to visit downtown Chicago." Kindly, that policeman showed us where to get an underground train, which we found and went downtown.

It was a long way, though we could not know where to stop. We were targeting the stop closest to the largest buildings.

On our way, I started telling my brother how The Work helped our minds to know the truth and compared different situations of life.

- The police didn't put us under mistreatment, but our minds did that on their behalf.
- The police didn't tell us what was going to happen to us, but our minds already were telling on their behalf.
- The police didn't tell us that we were going to jail, but our minds did that on their behalf.
- The police did not tell us that we were going to suffer; our minds repeatedly told us that on their behalf.

Who assigned our minds to do others jobs? "Fear!" was at the basis of everything. Because our minds were fearful, they were telling us all those negative legends and the "I" believed that. What could be the result when we believe our stressful thoughts? Sufferings! On the other hand we had our families in Rwanda and our minds were thinking on their behalf during that scenario.

My wife didn't tell me that she was going to miss me; rather my mind was representing the image of my wife screamingly saying to me, "I and your children are going to miss you."

When we believe our fearful minds, we can mistakenly live in deep confusion and even think on suicide.

We were glad to know the power of The Work: it was a good companion to both me and my brother during our long trip home to Rwanda.

Meanwhile, we were in downtown Chicago and found some of the items were very cheap compared to the prices in our home country. My brother, who was passionate for beer, couldn't avoid this. He found the Dutch beer Heineken at a cheap price and in very attractive cans of 16 ounces, so he grabbed three. I obtained one bottle of juice and that was enough for me. On the way back to the train station, we saw a public phone. We were engaged to call back home. My brother Leopold first called a friend and informed, "I am bringing to you Heineken beers in the smartest cans you have ever seen."

No chance was there to enter in the airport with our special gifts purchased in Chicago. I was the first to be told to throw my nice bottle of juice in the trash can. The following person was my brother Leopold who had in his hand a heavy plastic bag containing the Heineken beers.

He was told to throw them in the trash can. He sadly said, "I have the receipt for these beers." Indifferently, the security man told him to throw them in the trash can. I kindly resisted and asked them for an apology and to just let him go with his beers. I was trying to explain to them that he was not going to drink those beers either in the terminal or on board. Leopold told me to ask them if he could drink at some place to drink beers at the airport! One of the security guys accepted and showed him where he could sit. Leopold started drinking and finished the first can and when he wanted to open the second, the same security guy came and stopped him from drinking more and told him to throw the two remaining beers in the trash can. Leopold did so and became very frustrated.

There came another intervention of The Work on the statement, "I am frustrated because my beers were thrown away."

I asked him if he could allow doing the inquiry on that. He was lying down on a carpet and barely accepted it. His mind was connected to the beers in the trash can.

Some people who like beer might have a laughing thought on this unfolding situation.

So we went on with the inquiry since we had other two hours and a half to board.

He told me that he could not be the client rather the facilitator. I accepted to be the client with the statement, "My beers were thrown."

Leopold: Your beers were thrown, *Is that true?*

Costa: Yes!

Leopold: Your beers were thrown, *Can you absolutely know that it's true?*

Costa: Yes!

Leopold: *How do you react, what happens when you believe that thought your beers were thrown?*

Costa: I react negatively. I feel to be powerless vis-à-vis these American security guys. I feel to be annoyed. They do not care for other person's benefits.

Leopold: Who would you be without the thought *My beers were thrown?*

Costa: I would be thinking like that matter did not happen and feel peace in me. I would be living this "Present."

Leopold: Your beers were thrown. *Can you turn around that statement?*

Costa: I closed my eyes and held my breath little a bit and breathed, held it again and breathed then open my eyes.

My beers were not thrown: the genuine example there was that one beer was consumed.

The mind was just alarming that beers were thrown and forgetting to rejoice about the one that was consumed.

He laughed a lot and said, "At least I consumed that one beer and even if I would not drink that one, there was no other choice other than of throwing those beers in the trash can. My mind took me in that trash can and held me powerless with those beers there."

We flew from Chicago to Brussels and on the check-in point I lost my son's computer toy. I noticed that when I was already on the plane. It was okay and I did not turn much time to think about it since I knew much more about the truth and the power of The Work.

Most of the time when I am suffering and not taking time to question my mind, I am "*throwing flowers to that fearful mind*"—wrongly honoring it.

That would be like someone who has a wound and the mind will start telling him, "This wound is on a very dangerous part of the body; it will take much time to be healed," and the "I" believes that, as the result of sufferings.

> *The World is your perception of it. Inside and outside always match—They're reflections of each other. The World is the mirror image of your mind. If you experience chaos and confusion inside, your external world has to reflect that. You have to see what you believe, because you are the confused thinker looking out and seeing yourself…*" —Byron Katie, *Question Your Thinking, Change the World*

There is a power in me, which changes the way I believe. If I want to experience peace, I can experience peace; if I want to experience disarray, I can experience disarray.

It is the matter of knowing what I want to experience, what I will get out of that experience.

Even though we landed at Kigali airport in Rwanda I could not get out of there right away, and our last destination was Kampala, Uganda. Consequently, I was compelled to spend a night there and then in the morning take a bus from Kampala back to Kigali, Rwanda.

The following afternoon I arrived at home and my wife lovingly started commiserating about how many challenging situations I must have faced while being rerouted.

This is the way our minds always play with us. The mind can easily take you to a situation and assist you in living it.

The way I saw my wife, she was apprehensively rerouted already and suffering the same pain as someone who really was rerouted.

Where was the problem? Who was grieving for me having been rerouted? I remember when she was asking me how that happened; her face was representing a person who was even more tired than me. And that was different from giving me the warm welcome I needed.

The way we are attached to our stories can easily bring peace or grieving. When my mother saw me coming from jail in Congo, she fell sick. She was much more connected with my life in prison instead of enjoying "The Present," which was my release.

Since our minds can easily travel *without paying any ticket* to the past even far beyond to reach time before we were born, and imports stressful stories, actualizes them and convinces us to welcome them. When the "I" believes that, we live a traumatic outdated life experience: Suffering!

Here is what I observed in my family when this idea came from my mother's mind; she gathered us around her and said, "*Hutus are the foundation of our suffering, because in 1959 they killed our relatives and chased out your parents.*"

Immediately she had a headache and that night a hurtful sleep. In the morning she could not go to the market to do her business.

"The Present" peaceful time was also available then. My mother, my father and my aunt managed to escape and they survived. Praise God for that as well.

The past has also its beautiful moments. We can remember and import happy moments and celebrate them today. Just notice it.

*Conception is not reality.* —(Earl Grant from Faith Temple, July 12, 2010)

## ‹› CHAPTER 6 ‹›

# The Power of The Work

The School for The Work is neither a religion nor a political party. From its nature, The School is a "bay of freedom."

The way I grew up with my internal conflict, which was reproducing persistent pain and abhorrence day after day, I was totally living in profound confusion as my reality. I was supporting my mind by believing what my fearful mind was telling me.

What my mother was telling me was real and I had to abide with it. Since she was my mother, I did not know how to resist. My mother was much attached to her stories, which she was transferring to us.

We were taught that "*Our mothers are the bridges that God used to put us in this world.*"

The "I" extremely agreed with what I got from my mother. I went on by receiving and using her stressful stories. She thought to have peace when she narrated her hurtful past experience and saw me crying.

I can't wait for the environment response to make my peace. We often think peace can come when someone who hurt us asks for forgiveness and pleads guilty. Yes! It is human to ask for forgiveness, but what happens when that person who hurt me does not ask for forgiveness? If I think that by being told, "forgive me" that I can get inner peace, it means that I am controlled by that person.

Peace, happiness, love, hatred, conflict, they all have their origins in me. What I want them to bring in me is what I will create.

Several times, I was thinking that by wreaking vengeance against that Congolese soldier, Pongo, who put me in jail and left me to his colleagues for torture, I could be peaceful. Many times I told my mother, "*I will be peaceful after doing something bad to Pongo.*"

On the other hand, Pongo was holding my peace.

The first person I facilitated to do The Work was my mother, Martha. She is a person who likes joking and telling tales. However, all her jokes will go negatively to Helene the lady who was presumed to have witched my father, to the 1959 mass killing of Tutsis, to her life of exile and particularly to my records of being tortured and imprisoned. Several times she called me "*Mandela.*" After I completed my 2008 inquiry with the Work, I noticed that my mom was living with fear, and the results were hatred and conflict.

Two years after my father's death, my mom burned all things related to my father. The reason was that they were making her remember too much her lovely husband, Claver Ndayisabye. All clothes, which could have been recycled by some of us—shoes, papers—everything—were destroyed.

We rescued my father's framed picture and after she found out, my mother kept it far from sight in her briefcase. Why? She didn't want to see it; she was telling us that seeing the picture of someone she could not see, was hurtful.

For the past years and years I also believed the same, but The Work intervened and showed me how we were personifying that picture into the living death of our father.

With my Judge Your Neighbor Work Sheet designed by Byron Katie translated into Kinyarwanda by my wife Berna-dette, as well as the Yellow Card, I went to facilitate The Work with my mom.

She was ready for The Work.

I asked her, if we could put my father's picture up on the wall again. She told me that, "*My husband's picture can bring suffering into me.*"

Costa: "*My husband's picture can bring suffering into me,*" Is that true?

My mother: Yes!

Costa: "*My husband's picture can bring suffering into me.*" Can you absolutely know that it's true?

My mother: Yes!

Costa: How do you react, what happens, when you believe that thought; "*My husband's picture can bring suffering into me?*"

My mother: I do not want to see it. I just hide it far from me. I get goosebumps every time when I approach the briefcase where the picture is kept.

Costa: Who would you be without the thought, "*My husband's picture can bring suffering into me?*"

My mother laughed and laughed starting to bring out tears," then stood up and went to bring the picture.

She requested for me to hang it up. She rather found peace in that picture, which really reminds us how our father was a hero and lovely man in the whole society.

It is by interacting with your mind that you can really discover the truth. When I was writing the previous paragraph on July 17, 2010, I got a shock and lost my way. However, with the inquiry everything can work around to peace.

I had a phone call from Rwanda with news about my longtime pal who was much more like my brother to me. "*Silas Rwangeyo passed away.*" I immediately told my wife the news, and she fell into tears. Our son Gentil could not realize what was happening to us. Our daughter Queen so innocently crying by being attached to our thoughts.

An inquiry alarm came in my mind. I went in Gentil's bedroom and started doing The Work.

I talked to Silas three days before he passed away and I was making some kind of advocacy to help him find funds for placement in a higher experimental hospital. When I talked to him he told me, "I hope to be healed Costa." He was gone now and the inquiry was *Who is suffering now?* I was brokenhearted and felt weak by not having reached my goal of placing him in another hospital.

My lovely Silas had completed his journey and was peacefully resting somewhere and I couldn't have control over that. I was again and again in my inquiry. *It was just the beginning!*

I started realizing that, my mind was fearful by the news of Silas' death. Then I went on with the Turnaround, "*Silas is alive.*"

I needed to get some genuine examples on that in my mind in order to bring peace within me.

I can still hear Silas telling me some stories, especially the ones of pygmies he was always joking, such as:

> *Costa, one pygmy was called upon with a bad news that his son was hit by a vehicle. When he arrived at the accident field he found his son died. He was furious and the driver was fearful. The driver pulled out from his pocket a big amount of money and gave it to that pygmy whose son was killed. Seeing that big portion of money, the pygmy said to the driver, "Wait, I bring for you his brother," pretending to get more money!*

I left the room and told my wife Bernadette that Silas is still alive, because he can talk to me. I can even still see his face in my mind and interact with him. He is peaceful even more so than I am.

My wife said to me that she got into my e-mail inbox and saw many messages of sympathy, one of them from a lovely lady friend who even feels comfortable enough to call me her brother as I used to do. After having the news of Silas's peaceful trip, she sent this:

> *My Dear Brother,*
>
> *I write this with great sadness in my heart and tears in my eyes. I cannot find the words to express to you how sorry I am for the passing of this sweet and gentle soul. I know you did your best and never for a second did you fail him, I know that will bring you little comfort during this time, but be assured you were a true friend to him when he needed it most...*
> *Your loving Sister*

It is okay for me to live with the love my friends and relatives who passed away were providing me. Living with that is living with peace. At that time I experienced their presence in my mind in a peaceful way.

With the inquiry I could come with the idea of, "*When my friend or relative died,*" I get an alert, "*What did I do to help him?*" "*Tomorrow is my turn.*" Again another alert comes and says, "*You will die,*" or even, "*You are dying.*"

Remembering how helpful my father was to my family should be an opportunity for me to celebrate his bravery. "Silas" was lovely to me. Inside me I am still feeling his love.

One day I talked with a friend whose mother was at the last stage of her life. She said to me, "*Costa my friend, I am fretful of my mom's current life. She is on her last stage of her life.*"

While we were talking on the phone, I ran to open the book of Byron Katie called *Question Your Thinking: Change The World*, and read to her:

> *When you're clear about death, you can be totally present with someone who's dying, and no matter what kind of pain she appears to be experiencing, it doesn't affect your happiness. You're free to just love her, to hold her and care for her, because it's your nature to do that.*

*To come to that person in fear: she looks into your eyes
and gets the message that she's in deep trouble. But if
you come in peace, fearlessly, she looks into your eyes and
sees that whatever is happening is good.*

It is by questioning my mind that I can know the truth of
what is going on within me. My fearful mind needs interaction
to avoid suffering. It's in its nature to acquire facts and repro-
duce these to me.

When "I" believe, everything my mind tells me, happiness or painful results will appear in me. *"An owl is a bird that
causes curses."* Fearfully my mind imported that and put me on
attention. "I" believed. When I was seeing an owl I was treating the bird as the bearer of curses. Where was that reflection
reproduced? In me!

But if I noticed in my mind, *"An owl is a bird that causes
curses"* and went on with the inquiry, what could happen? The
truth! My mind loves me and provides many things for me to
deal with. However, there must be a good time of interaction
between the "I" and mind. Dialogue between the conscious and
unconscious mind can help me to balance and find out what is
going to bring peace and what is going to bring stress.

I was imagining the owl to be a cursed bird. After doing my
inquiry and starting to live with The Work, things were changing progressively and peacefully. I was then noticing the good
aspects of owls. I always have in my mind a very good challenging surprise I encountered in Greenville, South Carolina, when
I visited a friend named Laura K. Greiner. She gave me a room
and on the wall there was a beautiful picture of two owls fixing
their eyes on me. I could understand them in my imagination
communicating, *"We are friendly."*

Tearing up, in the morning I went to tell Laura how I
slept. She saw that there might be something that happened
to me. I said, "Laura, I heard owls talking to me and I was

considering them as bearers of curses. I had never thought that I could one day sleep where owls' pictures are but they told me that *they are friendly.*"

Laura started telling me how owls are very important to many communities. She said that there is a community which considers them as messengers. More to that, she said that one day an owl woke her up when she was sleeping. And it was really the time to wake up.

One day on a morning walk at my second School for The Work in 2009, I saw an owl on the parking building close to the Los Angeles airport and simultaneously pointing my finger I said, "*You are Costa.*" I deeply felt an inner peace in me.

On my way back from the morning walk, I got a paper and replaced the owl with one of the persons I was negatively considering from my past. That was the Congolese soldier, Pongo, who ordered me to be detained and tortured, when I was seventeen. I tried to write down some of the qualifications I was representing him with in my mind and then turned them around by giving one example for each.

> Pongo:
> You don't care,
> You're selfish,
> You're stupid,
> You're unhappy,
> You're my enemy,
> You're sadist,
> You're a killer.
> Costa:
> I don't care, when I accept to host hatred in me.

I'm selfish, when I always want Pongo to leave this World and not me.

I'm stupid, when I think I have power to control the outside.

I'm unhappy, when I choose to live stressfully.

I'm my enemy, by torturing my life hectically.

I'm sadist, by thinking on revenge and putting my life in a stressful status.

I'm a killer, by choosing the escape of suicide.

It is by rudely naming and qualifying our so-called enemies that we drop ourselves into confusion. That goes with hating everything that has a similarity or connection with those "enemies."

In March 2009, I met a friend and he wanted to write down his e-mail address for me; he borrowed a pen and when he started writing. He saw a label on that pen "Made in Germany," he immediately threw the pen and smashed it on the ground. I bowed and picked up the pieces of that poor pen. I wanted to know what was wrong with that pen. He told me that he did not use anything made from Germany. I got the invitation of going to their communities for my presentation, "The Work that Brings Peace in Me."

I travelled to their place and more people were in the room for the presentation. Before projecting my presentation, I told them, "I can see you are so beautiful people and bright." That was really my first perception, just when I entered in the room; I saw some of them were smiling.

I grabbed those pieces of that pen, which was victimized because it was bearing the label, "Made in Germany," and asked "How can we conflict with a pen because of its label?" A pen is unconscious since it doesn't hold any story about 1945.

Screamingly a lady stood up and said loudly, "Costa, my mom has told me to never drive a BMW, Mercedes Benz, VW, or other German brand cars." I asked her if she knew the reason. She said, "Due to the holocaust, it is immoral to drive those cars."

I took a yellow card with the four questions and I asked her if she was ready to do The Work. She accepted.

The statement was, "It is immoral to drive German made cars."

Costa: "*It is immoral to drive German made cars.*" Is it true?

She: Yes!

Costa: "*It is immoral to drive German made cars.*" Can you absolutely know that it's true?

She: No!

Costa: I invite you to close your eyes and answer this question. How do you react, what happens when you believe that thought, "*It is immoral to drive German made cars?*"

She: I feel so hateful in me and live with conflict. I can't even think of buying those cars.

Costa: Who would you be without the thought, "*It is immoral to drive German made cars?*"

She: I could not think at all to that confusion [crying and hugging me].

Costa: "*It is immoral to drive German made cars.*" Can you turn around that statement and give genuine examples?

She: I am immoral.

Those cars don't know anything about my suffering.

I have a friend who wanted to give me a ride in a VW Jetta and I refused.

Costa: Another Turnaround?

She: It is not immoral to drive German made cars.

I know many nice people who drive German made cars.

BMW always seems to be cute to me.

Costa: "*It is immoral to drive German made cars.*" Is it true?

She: No!

Things are beautiful: the environment including the surroundings, creeks, birds, lakes, oceans . . . .

It isn't just when I have a peaceful mind that I can realize nice melodies from creeks, trees, oceans, birds, the earth?

I will start hating them when I hate myself. Things are just what I want them to be. There are many things that we picture them to be part of our suffering. I was feeling as if I hated all Congolese because of Sergeant Pongo who arrested and tortured me.

The realization of my stressful mind will create unfair treatment of this beautiful environment.

It is when I got into trouble with my counterpart that I would think to find "*Peace*" by killing the dog, breaking chairs, committing suicide.

## ⁊ CHAPTER 7 ⁊

# Community Self-inquiry Experiences "The Work"

After my first School for The Work in 2008 I tried to apply my experience to my community.

Even though I felt as if I knew the truth, I noticed that there was still doggedness on the side of my fearful mind. I knew that fear is one of the most common ailments in the globe. When fear is using the mind, there is an alarm telling me, "Be careful."

However, by questioning my fear-intoxicated mind, I can realize that the wrongness is not from the outside but rather in me. That is truth.

> *"The Work transforms difficulties to opportunities."* —Lucy Dunlap, Greenville, South Carolina

My community faced conflict for a long time, even today. Some persistent atrocities are still committed by people who are much attached to their stories. As for my experience, I knew how much The Work can be requisite to heal wounds related to our past.

Some of the people who experienced severe atrocities in the past are my wife Bernadette and her siblings, Yves and Denise.

Yves was so curious to know The Work and how someone could go with it. When I was facilitating The Work in different homes, I used to go with him and he was internally doing his inquiry. I remember one day he told me, "I am ready to hold the yellow card and help those who want to do the inquiry." He added saying that The Work is a "*pain downloader.*"

However, Bernadette failed several times to finish her inquiry and she ended up screaming in pain. When that happened to her, I got into tears as well. I asked one of my friends familiar with The Work what I could do to help my wife live more peacefully. She answered me, "Do The Work on that." I decided to go for another School in 2009. I was lucky to again receive a scholarship. That was my amazing time with The Work. I was enjoying The Work and felt I was traveling in another world full of peace.

During my stay in the Crowne Plaza, I had my roommate Richard, who seemed to be very familiar with The Work and, by being released from my own sorrows, I could easily share what was going on. On the first day we introduced ourselves to each other in our room and I told him that I came to School for the second time because of the suffering my wife was experiencing. I said, "I failed several times to help her to do The Work. When she cried, I cried!"

Richard was very wise; he was just listening, and by the end of my overview he said, "Good for you."

The last day, I felt full of power within me and understood much more reality on the inquiry process. Richard invited me to have lunch together. I said, frankly, "I don't have money." I knew that I have to be careful with North Americans and even Europeans. I have been experiencing their culture, which is very different from an African's. You can be invited for lunch, dinner or a drink in a restaurant and after consumption you can be told to share the bill! Outside the room, my friend Sarah and Genevieve were uncomplainingly waiting for me when I was arranging everything. Richard told me, "I am going to offer you and your friends."

While seated for lunch, Richard asked me, "How was The School?" I replied saying that all my nine days were much more focused on how I failed to help my wife to complete her inquiry. I knew that it was so difficult to help her to do The Work effectively, while myself I was still attached to her story. "When she cried, I also cried!" I realized that I needed to be peaceful to facilitate The Work.

My second School for The Work was kind of a deep revelation to me. I knew that from our problem grows love. From our screams derive our smiles. I was invited to meet a friend of mine in Nevada City, California, Jill Fox Caruthers, who actually hosted me and my Rwandan fellows in Beverly Hills prior to our first school in 2009. I did two presentations there. Then I went to the east coast of the USA for further presentations on how we need to treat ourselves as caregivers. Thus, when we are peaceful, our clients will harvest from our peace.

Back in Rwanda I thought about the process called, "The Work in your Home." This involved fixing an appointment and facilitating the in-house inquiry.

I tried that and it was successfully done when I facilitated my mother to do her inquiry. The process is less expensive since it is conducted at zero cost. On the other hand, it was tiresome as it required traveling some long distances by walking. But after the inquiry there was always a smile, peace. I forgot all the tiredness of the walk, through the happiness that emanated from finding the source of peace inside us and not outside.

After having that opportunity to go into myself and *download* many things that I was senselessly keeping, I decided to go to different areas to spread my love using my PowerPoint presentation.

My first presentation was organized in my church in Kigali, Rwanda. The church was full and the special people who were invited were "Women Living with HIV/AIDS." The reason to focus on that category of people was the way I was seeing them living anxiously. That was the result of our past beliefs, "Being HIV positive is to get to the door of death." Others were sorrowful with the stigma that was boorishly used against them.

My heart was then beating in a strange manner. I was striving to tell them I was released from past stories but also fighting with my mind, which was telling me, "Eh! Are you going to tell everybody that you were imprisoned in three countries?" But, "I" was committed to do so. That is "The Present."

I remember Byron Katie used to say, "This is just the beginning," and every moment of the inquiry is new.

As is my custom, I always start by introducing "The Work," then my personal experiences. We got denied the projector at the last moment, so I verbally reproduced my presentation, "The Work that Brings Peace in Me." People were crying in the room to hear my stories. However, after telling them how much I suffered in the past, I went on by presenting how The Work wiped out all the suffering and I felt cleaned up. I could hear in the room people saying, "*Yoooooooo!*" which in other countries can mean, "oh no!" I couldn't feel anymore that my life was spoiled.

I told the participants how we suffer from our stories by keeping them posted into our daily lives and considering them as real, present facts.

Since people said that being HIV positive means, "The door to death, miserable life and just sorrowful ideas" and the "I" believes, what happens? Suffering! It is by questioning our minds that we can have the chance to know the truth. Those who consider HIV/AIDS to mean death and a miserable life were just fearful. It is simply by being peaceful in my heart that

I can easily prevent others from being infected by HIV stigma. It is by being peaceful that I can stop spreading HIV discrimination and protect myself from being miserable. This occurs with doing the inquiry again and again and learning the truth on how to live serenely and hopefully with HIV. Fear is the basis of our suffering. I was living for more than twenty years with my stories. During those years I couldn't reveal to people what happened to me, but I was living with constant suffering in me.

By keeping anger and stress in us, we are ruining our source of peace and sometimes living miserably. After explaining all the process of The Work of Byron Katie and my experience, an HIV positive lady stood up and screamingly told me that she would like to be assisted to do the inquiry. We did two big circles since the room was small and we were about two hundred people.

We had the four questions plus the Turnaround in Kinyarwanda. She was so brave and really curious. The Work started.

She came up with the statement, "*HIV is the cause of my misery.*"

Costa: "*HIV is the cause of my misery.*" Is it true?

She: Yes!

Costa: "*HIV is the cause of my misery.*" Can you absolutely know that it's true?

She: Yes!

Costa: "*HIV is the cause of my misery.*" How do you react, what happens, when you believe that thought?

She: I suffer; I just lay in my bed. My children will not find food that day, because I will not go to do my business of selling tomatoes.

Costa: "*HIV is the cause of my misery.*" Who would you be without the thought?

She: I can't be without that thought because I live with HIV and I know that.

Costa: Just imagine being without the thought. Represent yourself in that situation whereby you don't have that thought.

She: That could be a peaceful situation. My two children could be having food and lovely care from their mom.

Costa: "*HIV is the cause of my misery.*" Can you turn that thought around? Then give some genuine examples.

She: I am the cause of my misery. [*she was smiling*]

When I have the thought I don't go for my job.

When I suffer I become lazy and weak.

I became Christian when I was tested HIV positive.

Costa: Another Turnaround and example?

She: HIV is not the cause of my suffering.

I know the truth. I am the cause of my suffering. I will work hard. Smiling, she ran and went to hug one of the participants tightly.

The room was full of tears and happiness. The large number of participants, hands on their cheeks, and following the steps curiously and passionately.

What we think to be the truth by stressfully accepting that way of living will always be wrong. It is not necessary to live daily in mental anguish. When any situation brings stress to me I now take time to question my mind. I take The Work (TW) like food. I am hungry. I need food. I am anxious, I need TW.

Everyone deserves love, peace, and happiness. I remember one day a lady came to my house and she was asserting to my wife that HIV is ruining her life. I asked her how? She told me that she is thirty years old and only weighs 45kgs (99 lbs). I told her I have my cousin's sister, who is not HIV positive, is forty years old and only weighs 45kgs (99 lbs).

## Today

*Love my body the way it is, today*
*Suffering can't allow me to cater to my body, today!*
*Happiness is the only way to cater to my body, today!*
*My body is hurting today!*
*Who is telling me that my body is hurting,*
*my body is hurting, today!?*
*The other friend of mine that is my mind who loves me today!*
*Does the wounded area really hurt today!?*
*Something's wrong with my mind, something's*
*wrong at this time, today!*
*You are not wrong my mind, but you sing a fearful song, today!*
*Be strong, turn on the right direction, and be peaceful, today!*
*By questioning you, my mind, I'm helping me, today!*
*Love my body the way it is, today!*

# CHAPTER 8

# The Work that Brings Peace in Me

In a normal job situation most people need to work in order to get their salary. They will be sweating for hours but by the end of the course they will have their salary and rejoice. The Work of Byron Katie was to me like a real job. Who is the employee and the boss during The Work? I am both. The Work is about me and the salary is the result obtained after the inquiry. By exercising it, I was discovering a peaceful way to the truth, which is always there but covered by my fearful mind.

After being in several meetings presenting my awakened situation, "The Work that Brings Peace in Me," I decided to make a video documentary, which had the same name as my PowerPoint presentation. In April 2009, I held a one-day workshop in the community where I talked about The Work of Byron Katie, how it helped me to discover the reality of my life and focus much more on The Present. After the workshop, which was conducted outside under beautiful green trees, I passed a communiqué asking if there was any person willing to do The Work in Your Home, which could be videotaped. Many hands were up so we did a quick lottery and selected two.

I fixed an appointment with a first lady who was suffering for a long time from severe trauma. Her first husband died and the second she married was imprisoned.

Her son was almost three years passed away, two days before the date we fixed for The Work in her home. The blame of the death of her son went to the neighbor. The child was buried in her yard.

She resisted doing the inquiry and was in deep distress. She couldn't even look at the grave which was covered by weeds. She told how much she was angry with her neighbor because she *witched* her son. She added saying, "*Look where I am living and just close to my son's grave. I can't talk to him. It is very hurtful for me to see what my neighbor did to my son and my family as a whole.*"

I asked her if she was ready to do the inquiry on her son's death; she barely accepted. I told her that it was just an invitation for her to discover the truth that could bring peace in her and to her family.

She produced a statement, "My neighbor killed my son." We went through all four questions of the inquiry, arriving at the Turnaround, and she said, "I killed my son," and I asked her if she had any situation where she thought to do so. She said, "*I didn't take him to the hospital when he fell sick.*" I asked her again, "Your neighbor killed your son." Is it true? She smiled and didn't respond. The accused neighbor was following from nearby all the time we were spending there. I requested of her if we could invite her neighbor. She said, "Yes, but *I don't know that she can come.*" We called the neighbor and she came. They hugged each other lovingly.

It is by doing The Work that you can do things with a spirit of reconciliation and unity. After the Inquiry, the lady was open and realized that due to the sorrowful situation she was living with, she couldn't even talk on her son's grave. But she was willing to go with me and together we started removing all the weeds from the grave. She was doing that peacefully.

There comes the significance of questioning our mind. It offers food for thought and we need to chew.

*"The only way I can support you, is to disagree with you."* —Mary, Edmonton, Alberta Canada

That was really my experience before doing my inquiry to stop dwelling on the facts that negatively affected my life. My wife couldn't even go to Kibuye, the place she was born in, grew up in, and survived the 1994 Tutsis' Genocide in.

One day I asked her, "What would be your answer if our son Gentil asked you: 'Mom why don't you want to go to *the village where you were born?*" She couldn't respond to me. I knew she was having a battle within her. That was my experience and of many others. When we have something that is appearing to challenge our mind, a very quick alert will come and tell us to be ready. Fear! Fear!

Bernadette hated everything with a red color because it had something in connection with blood, which represented a picture of war and death in her mind. Before my School for The Work I was really supporting her idea not to buy or wear a red cloth. After having the opportunity to question my mind, a friend from Canada brought me a red t-shirt and presented it as a tool to help my mind go into her inquiry. She hardly wore it.

I always told her, "*Do your best to meet things you are afraid of, as one way of knowing the truth.*" Our stories are the real bridges that our fearful minds use to make our life better or worse. It is just by inquiry that the better can be separated from the worse.

When I am meeting people, I sometimes tell them that the only bad thing I've ever faced in my life was when I went to jail and the only good thing I've ever faced was being released from jail. All depends on my own way of naming things. We can name our stories with stressful names. At that time, our minds will start to bring to us some of the worst events that happened to us and completely cover the happiness met during our past and in being alive today.

In November 2009, I invited some friends and colleagues from The School for The Work to come volunteer to facilitate an inquiry. I called that event "Make Your Peace." Seven friends came from different parts to help. While we were conducting a half-day introduction to The School for The Work of Byron Katie, in our church were more than fifty women living with HIV attentively following; the participants showed an understanding of the four questions constituting The Work of Byron Katie. However, the Turnaround was a blocking point. No one wanted to Turnaround her statement. That was also my case when Byron Katie was assisting me to do my inquiry in the room in 2008.

Pamela Grace, one of the volunteers from Seattle who was named by Mom, *Umutoni,* *"Rwandan name given to a person to care with extreme love in the family,"* noticed how much the participants were struggling with the Turnaround so she gave them a peaceful example.

> *If you have a scar on your hand, don't forget to turn your hand and see on the other side how beautiful your palm is.*

In the room, the participants were enraptured by the truth of The Present. One of the participants was very touched by Pamela's contribution, which really also became one of my engine oils when I reached the Turnaround level.

My wife was taking the Turnaround like a fact of bearing responsibility for all the hurtful experiences she passed through. However, I discovered the Turnaround as a *"diplomatic proof of what my mind is trying to convince me."*

When we don't do the Turnaround, our inquiry isn't complete. It is like building a house and not entering it. Why build it? When you go with questioning your mind, *Is it true? Can you absolutely know it's true? How do you react, what happens, when you believe that thought? Who would you be without the thought?* Then you enter in your new house through the Turn-around and start living the peaceful present life.

The examples that derive from Turnaround trigger feelings of happiness that chase out all the sorrowful stories.

My wife said to me one day, "Our land is mistreated in Kibuye but due to the worst experiences I passed through in that area, I couldn't go there."

I beseeched her to come down and do the inquiry on that and see what evolved. It is very difficult to predict the outcome of The Work Process without going through it. She accepted to do The Work on that!

*"I have hurtful memories of Kibuye."*

Costa: *"I have hurtful memories of Kibuye."* Is it true?

Bernadette: Yes!

Costa: *"I have hurtful memories of Kibuye."* Can you absolutely know that it's true?

Bernadette: "Yes. My siblings and my parents were innocently killed there."

Costa: *"I have hurtful memories of Kibuye."* Who would you be without the thought?"

Bernadette: Peaceful. I would love Kibuye without stress.

Costa: *"I have hurtful memories of Kibuye."* Can you turn that around? Then give some examples?

Bernadette: I don't have hateful feelings of Kibuye.

I have never had a nice environment in Rwanda like where I was living.

My childhood was very magnificent in Kibuye.

I will never forget the beauty of our school ESI Mugonero in Kibuye, where I went for my high school studies.

The first food I liked in my life I ate in my parents' home in Kibuye.

I like the weather of Kibuye, close to Lake Kivu.

(She was peaceful while giving the examples of the Turn-around. I could see her heart open, by her beautiful smile.)

Costa: Another Turnaround?
Bernadette: I have hurtful memories of me.
My mind was fearful.

Bernadette became cleared with her mind and found that Kibuye had done nothing wrong to her.

She was very brave and one day ten months later went with me to Kibuye and visited many places she had lived before, especially where their house was before the Tutsis' Genocide.

### I love you even if you think I don't love you!

*Lovely Turnaround. Ndayisabye N. Costa*
*Your Statement (...love you, even if you think you don't love me.) my lovely Sister Jeanette is so sweet to TURNAROUND.*
*Jeanette Stephens*
*...love you, even if you think you do love me.*
*...love you, even if I think you don't love me.*
*...love you, even if I think I don't love me.*
*....love you, even if I think I don't love you.*
*...love me, even if I think you don't love me.*
*Jeanette Stephens*
*Thank you, sweet brother, Costa!*
*Emily Goodman*
*Wow! Those were BEE-U-Tiful Turnarounds! Thank you both :)*

# The Work Toward Self-Reconciliation

As we're doing our own inquiry, we consciously go into a self-reconciliation. We many times believe something like, "If he doesn't ask me for forgiveness I won't forgive him." That is being driven by the outside, which we don't have the authority to control. That causes anger which is just destroying lives.

Some of the statements that we can undertake when we are stressful are:

- She needs to ask for forgiveness.
- He was wrong and he has to ask for forgiveness.
- I can't talk to him, he is mistaken.
- She needs to bow down before I give any help.
- If he doesn't come to me, he will suffer.

After completing my video documentary, I started sharing with my community and people began taking the time to question their minds to see if their stressful stories were bringing them peace or hatred. I do believe that we don't have to forget our stories; rather we can use them to make ourselves peaceful. I do believe in forgiving, not forgetting, because those who forget the past are destined to repeat it. The question for now is how much are my stories influencing or even controlling my life right now? That is story management.

Once, on my way to share with Burundians who experienced atrocities within their communities in the past, I met one of the sons of the policeman who arrested me. I was very curious to talk to him. Peacefully, I whistled and he looked back. He stopped and I went to him and I said, "I am so sorry your daddy passed away without my meeting him and asking for forgiveness." He said, "Why?" I told him to forgive me because my mind was extremely accusing him of being the source of my suffering. I gave him a copy of my video documentary and he was happy to hear that. I intended to go to meet the family of

Sergeant Pongo in Democratic Republic of Congo and even do my presentation in the area, but due to the war that was going on there I did not make it there. I decided to write a letter to them asking for forgiveness for my long-time vengeful thoughts.

Then it came to pass that I embarked on my campaign to spread The Work that Brings Peace in Me to North America in response to my friends' invitations.

It was so amazing to see how people I was meeting were awakened. But still the problem is that so many so often expect peace from "the outside."

In my language there is an encouraging proverb which says, "Neighbor's intervention always comes after a storm."

We don't have to wait for time, family status, and people, to be peaceful. If we think so, which situation are we in now?

Therefore be grateful for every minute you live and share with somebody "special things" about someone who hurt you and find peace inside yourself. As the outside isn't waiting for us, why should we wait for and believe in external facts? I can question my mind and see if the inner peace will really appear in me when:

- I get married!
- My wife gets her peace? Or my husband shows me true love?
- I live with you! Or I divorce from you!
- My parents care! Or my child obeys! My car is paid!
- I have a brand new car!
- I have a job; one, two, three ...jobs?
- I retire! Or remain with my job!
- I lose weight! Or I gain back my weight!
- I'm in winter! I'm in spring! I'm in summer! I'm in autumn!
- There is no turbulence!

The second minute from now is more unmanageable than this one. This is the happiest moment to rejoice in. NOW!

It is when I am waiting for outside developments, pretending to have a peaceful life, that I become too dependent, instead of being confident, creating my inner peace.

We have the power that we should use to know where true peace is. Living The Present is getting ready to cross the river Now. It will be like a myth-dream of waiting for the river to pass so that you can cross at a dry space.

One night before I did one presentation with a community of African Americans, I meditated a lot on what my mind might be if I was a member of that community. My mind was in deep confusion.

I told my mind that when I wake up I don't find someone to wash my body or brush my teeth. I don't need someone to tell me, "It is time to wash your body and brush your teeth."

The aim of washing is to be clean and avoid disease that can result from being dirty. However, when I am much stressed, I can't wash my body. I remember one time I spent three weeks without washing. I was seeing everything as useless. No one could do that for me. It was my business to take care of my body.

That is the same thing when we are looking for the way to find peace. The exercise should be undertaken by me. Peace is in me and no one can get inside me to help find out my peace. It is my business to do so.

Peace, cheerfulness, and realization are mine when I want to embrace them. This can be achieved by identifying my stressful thoughts within me and making full inquiry on them. The empowering process of The Work will help me realize my full potency through the powers of imagination, words, self-assurance, goal-setting, focus, determination, action, and love. People can notice miracles being created in them.

In the morning when I went in the room for my presentation, I found a large number of people waiting to hear what *"The Work That Brings Peace in Me"* is!

Before I presented my PowerPoint, which was already projected on the screen, I invited the participants to hear what I meditated on the night before and what the findings were.

I was curious as well to know what they thought.

"Whose task is the washing of my body?" They all said that is a personal care. I went on.

Whose business is it when I am hungry? The answer from them was, "My business."

Whose business is it when I am grieving? They looked at each other shaking heads, uncertain.

Whose business is it when I live peacefully? One bravely said, "It's my business."

After those questions we went on deeply with meditation together and we were trying to question our minds to identify stressful thoughts that we don't consider as our business.

We all noticed that, "When I am full of hatred, or anxious, there is something wrong between me and my mind." In order to have a very good peaceful way, I can question my mind.

## What Do I Have?

This question above came to me powerfully during meditation. It was part of my revelation after The School for The Work. It often comes to me since I went through the process of The Work of Byron Katie and was revealing the true fact of things I am uselessly keeping.

What do I have?

What I have, is what my children will be grabbing from me.

What I have, is what my friends can get from me.

*I may not be rich, but I can give what I have,*
*even if it is only TIME or to share a smile with someone*
*who others seem to look through.* —Kristina Grant,
*"You Just Have to Look,"* Faith Temple, Maine

In January 2010, I was among people who were invited to do a short presentation at an annual banquet organized by a humanitarian organization in San Francisco. The room was decorated and I could imagine how the hearts of organizers were. Peaceful! My speech was brief, and I said, "I got a chance to be imprisoned in three countries. But that is a story and I now live *The Present* which is all about peace. I got the simple opportunity to discover that everyone is worthy of questioning one's mind through the four questions."

The same month, I embarked to Canada. When I arrived at the airport luggage check-in counter, the security officer found my video documentary in my briefcase. She read the text on the back cover and was anxious.

She asked me, "Why were you arrested three times in three countries?"

I replied, "Because I met fearful people who were much attached to their stories."

She asked me, "You didn't do anything to be arrested and detained?"

I said, "I didn't face any trial."

She said, "You didn't do anything?"

I smiled, "I can't blame myself!"

She asked me, "Why are you smiling?"

I replied, "Those are just stories!"

She asked me, "So that didn't happen to you?"

I responded, "Yes, many years ago. Different from today's reality."

She asked me, "What is the reality in your documentary?"

I replied, "We always minimize The Present, and rely on our stories of which many of them are stressful. It's about my real life. The Present one!"

She asked me, "What do you come to do in Canada?"

I answered, "Spread loves, by sharing with people how to find peace by bringing our fearful minds to the table of self-inquiry" (She was now shaking her head up and down!) She ended up by asking me for the DVD. In one of her e-mails I received, she told me that she was going into herself much more, trying to find out the truth in her. My friends, who were outside the airport waiting for me, were wondering if I was still coming or not. While walking toward the exit door, I got a flash inside me, "Everyone wants to live peacefully."

While I was in Canada I got the opportunity to talk to different groups of people who experienced different kinds of conflicts. I presented to immigrants, to Canadian youth, to a branch of the University of British Columbia in Vancouver and to some First Nations Communities.

Prior to my presentation of *"The Work that Brings Peace in Me"* I invited the participants to think deeply on the question: "What do I have?"

The example was very simple:

*Let's say you bought a very nice cupboard from the Edmonton Mall and you install it in your home.*

*The cupboard will start having its beauty depending on the stuff that will be put in it. If you put in that cupboard nice fruits, delicious donuts, gorgeous flowers, nice decorated plates or cups, everyone will appreciate that cupboard. The first look will be positively flashed to someone's mind.*

*Your children, your guests, who will go to get something from that cupboard will be very happy viewing its magnificent reserve!*

*What can be the children's or friends' reaction if they find you put rotten fruits in your your cupboard? Your children*

*might be infected by that poor fruit and you could be in charge
of taking them to the hospital.*
  *What do I have?*

Your life deserves peace and not conflict, hatred or anxiety.
From that example, you can take a self-invitation to consider
yourself and see what you have.

From our depression, we breastfeed our children the same
things we have experienced, or even possibly what our great
grandparent's parents experienced. We give our children what
we have put in our cupboard, because that is what we have.
How can a spirit of forgiveness be part of my life if I still use
my stories as today's tool for life?

After the presentation of my PowerPoint, with some
examples from my personal experience, one of the First Nations
groups, told me, "My son was badly educated by my wife who
narrated to him everything bad that happened to our people
and since then my son is full of bad manners. He can't spend an
hour without anxiously talking about what the Europeans did to
his ancestors; he lives with hatred. From that belief my son has
even given up on his studies."

I quizzed him in the room, "Who is suffering today?"

He said, "I feel so bad with that every day." I asked,
"Why? He said, "My son's life is causing me a painful situation." I invited him to come in front of the others. He bravely
joined me. I asked him, "Your son's life is causing you a painful
situation, is that true?"

He said, "Of course!"

I asked, "Can you absolutely know that it's true, 'your
son's life is causing you a painful situation?'"

He said, "Yeah!"

I continued, "Your son's life is causing you a painful situation?" How do you react, what happens, when you believe that
thought?

He said, "I feel so sad and I don't want to see him and my wife."

I asked him, "Does that bring peace or stress in you?"

He emphasized, "Much stress!"

I asked him, "Your son's life is causing you a painful situation." Who would you be without the thought?

He said, "I couldn't feel this sadness! I couldn't be as stressful as I am!"

(His community members were following that with much attention and as we were proceeding with The Work, the silence was turning into tears).

I invited him, to find a Turnaround of "Your son's life is causing you a painful situation."

He started smiling in the room and everyone one was laughing.

I invited him to lower or completely close his eyes and find a Turnaround on that thought.

He said, "I am causing my life to be in a painful situation!"

He gave an example by saying; "I didn't prevent it when his mom started to tell him that the first time. I remember I was telling his mom such news I got from my grandfather." (He ran back to his seat and started crying.)

I shared with the participants an example of my family.

My mom was fearful and her mind was providing her pure confusion. After becoming a widow, she was wondering how to survive. Her mind was telling her that "things are over." She gathered us and said, "All our suffering was caused by Hutus." We believed so. Our life was becoming poorer and poorer, especially when she was grieving.

That is what I always told my wife. *"You lost your parents and siblings during the Tutsis' Genocide and by the grace of God you and your two siblings survived. When you get anxious, do The Work and inquire if the moment you are in is appropriate. When you are peaceful, you can explain to your children, Gentil and*

*Queen Byron, what happened to their grandparents and uncles. That can be helpful to them, even to know that what happened was inhumane and that you don't wish them to minimize or to do the same thing those fearful killers did."*

She could only do that when she passed her own inquiry and saw where today's reality is. She always told me that her parents and my siblings' deaths have intensely affected her life—that went with a mental crisis, hatred and persistent grieving.

Our fearful mind is much connected to our mistakes and false realizations. I don't believe that our parents, relatives, friends, who passed away "are wishing for us to live miserably."

*When you have suffering the following steps can be undertaken:*
1. *What is wrong with me? This question will help you just to know that there is something that is not normal in you.*
2. *Invite your mind and make friends with it.*

As someone useful in the community and family, it can be a very valuable action to take time and question your mind on whatever fact you think is the source of your misery. Self-peace will become a communal and family peace.

When the presentation session was over, all the participants came to hug me and they were asking me how they could get the four questions. I gave my yellow card with four questions to the man who completed the inquiry on *"My son's life is causing me a painful situation."* He told me, "We relied a lot on our stories and that causes us to be even much more dependent. I will no longer be dependent. I want to work for myself and my family."

As you can't plant corn intending to harvest sorghums, it is the same thing that will happen to our children. What you sow is what you are going to reap. If you are full of conflict, that is what your children will be getting from you.

There is a lovely lady, a friend of mine who lives in Canada, with whom I have been exchanging some inquiry experiences.

She always asks me how The Work of Byron Katie has helped me to change my life.

When she knew that I was in Canada she called me and asked, "Costa, advise me. My husband wants to divorce me and I don't want my son to grow up within his mind that his parents divorced."

I didn't feel ready to respond to her at that very moment. She was asking curiously and intensely.

I told her to write that down and we could talk about it later. She kept insisting, saying, "Today!"

I said, "Yes! Today!"

In the evening time, before I went to a presentation, I called her. She answered and asked, "Can we talk now?"

"Yes," I replied.

She reproduced to me the same sentence, "My husband wants to divorce me and I don't want that. My son will be growing up with hatred."

I told her to hold the four questions and do The Work on "My son will be growing up with hatred."

At the end of The Work, she realized that she was the problem and not her son. Her son wasn't connected to her stories.

She gave a Turnaround that brought her peace. "*I am going to be living with hatred.*" The example she gave was, "*I hate my husband for having chosen to divorce.*"

I continued with her along these lines:

My children are wonderful and don't even believe the same way I do. They are born without any story and live profoundly in The Present. They start unknowingly breastfeeding from our nerve-racking reflections and when they believe them they go the same way of their parents. If you ask my son Gentil today, "What is a snake?" He will say, "Satan," but when he was six months old he could have even touched it.

By intentionally transferring, stressfully, our so-called *"Love"* to our children, we are also suffering from self-destructive behavior.

Then I told her, "Before and after divorce, there could be good times for inquiry to each of the decisions that we are going to undertake." Which one is going to bring peace, and which is going to bring stress? How to know this? Inquire! It will be peaceful if you complete your inquiry: it can be stressful when you start representing the outside as the root cause of your suffering.

The inquiry will be successfully done when you can stop blaming others as the agents of your stressful stories.

*"Are you concerned because you want me to succeed?"*

Why are you living in this stressful situation? Because of:
- My ex-husband/my wife.
- My children/my parents.
- My sister/my brother.
- My government/my community.
- My boyfriend/my girlfriend.
- My church/my school.

We can only have the ability to change our stressful stories to an unconditional love if we can inquisitively interact with our minds.

> *"When they believe their thoughts, people divide reality into opposites. They think that only certain things are beautiful. But to a clear mind, everything in the world is beautiful in its own way."* —Byron Katie/ Stephen Mitchell, *A Thousand Names for Joy*

# Twin Inquirer Boxes (TIB)

There is a way we can classify our stories when they are bringing anxious states to us. Do we really know when they happened? I got an experience in one of my meditations with the "Twin Inquirer Boxes." The TIB helped me and those I have met in various places, to not be attached to our stories, which doesn't mean to forget, rather not to use them as our "curriculum."

I used TIB for myself as a game to locate my stories and show my mind what we are dealing with and where we are. Most of the time when I finish helping my wife to do The Work, we take time to relax and do the TIB game.

The first time I did the TIB game outside of my family was during my one-day workshop with Native Americans in the United States.

Forty-five people came to participate. Different from Rwanda or Burundi where I have been introducing The Work of Byron Katie, all the participants were men. There wasn't even a single woman in the room.

While we were waiting to start, I was interacting with some of them outside the workshop room.

They were asking me, which country I was from. I said, "Rwanda," and I asked them if they had ever heard about Rwanda. They told me that Rwanda was known by everyone in 1994. That was during the Tutsis' Genocide. They were curious to know if I was there during that time, I responded, "Find a lot in my presentation." One of them told me, "We experienced the same here in North America." Yes! I said. Sufferings can be from different sources of fear and they are the same. Sufferings! Sufferings!

In the room, I shared with the participants the process of The Work, guided with the four questions plus the Turn-around and the Judge Your Neighbor Work Sheet. I projected my PowerPoint presentation.

Fifteen minutes before breaking, I introduced to them the TIB game. I gave each a blank sheet of paper and invited them to the first step of the TIB game, which is meditation. Then the second step was to sort out from our stories the one which brings us anxious and sorrowful thoughts that affect our lives. I could see everybody was very concentrated on the paper.

When we finished writing, I brought two boxes. One was called "The Story" and the second was called "The Present." Inside "The Story" box, there was a label that could read "stress" and inside the "The Present" box, there was a label that could read "peace."

The time for break was up, and the last step of the TIB game was there. Read the letter in silence, two minutes meditation and then put it in its appropriate box with curiosity of reading what was written on the inside label. I invited two people to volunteer reading what they wrote. I was the first volunteer and we had another one.

My letter was about the guy who told me outside that he knew Rwanda because of the Genocide. I was wondering why not on the peace and the reconciliation process that has been undertaken there? My heart was breaking trying to understand people still having in their minds Genocide and not all the peace that is prevailing among the hearts of Rwandans in these current times.

When I was reading there was a silence in the room and everyone was attentively following.

After reading my letter, I proceeded with meditation. I put my letter in its appropriate box which was "The Story." What was inside? Stress! When you still have in your mind Rwanda equals to Genocide, you are outdated and living stressful when you have that consideration. Today Rwanda is a beautiful and peaceful country.

The second person who came after me, started to read his letter which was much related to what happened to Native

Americans. He couldn't finish it and he went to put his paper in the "The Story" Box. He finished by going outside crying.

The exercise was done in silence and individually. Forty-two out of forty-five participants managed to do that and three resisted.

When we came back in the workshop room, the three who resisted wanted to know what was written inside the box. I allowed them to go and see what was inside the box. They found the truth. When we keep good memories they are always for maintaining the happiness we have experienced in the past, and when we are keeping stressful thoughts, we are experiencing the same suffering in that certain current moment. There the third question of The Work intervenes, "How do you react, what happens, when you believe the thought?" That is very clear. Believing is different from forgetting. You can still remember that and not believe that. It is not the reality for today. It was the reality of that time.

There is no place in us to accommodate affliction until we want to find a place for it. However, when a mind becomes scared, it is mistakenly actualizing those stressful stories. We revisit and we represent that inside us.

I look at a ripe apple on the tree and my mouth is full of saliva.

I look at that lobster and my mouth is full of envy.

Where is the problem there? Is it that apple? Is it that lobster? Or, it's my mind! It tells me, "That apple or that lobster is delicious." When I believe, other resentments follow.

That is the same way we get a mirror image from our stories. My mind tells me to look at my scars. If I was not tortured, my skin would be clean and smooth. When I believe that, all the components of my past suffering come back and I will start experiencing the same suffering in me again. The truth behind that is covered by my anguish. My scars, my stories don't talk. I talk on their behalf by making them revive in me. In that case I can choose which story to revive.

I always tell my wife to tell us stories on how her father was caring for her. When she is narrating these, I can feel peace in me. And my son Gentil, will be saying, "I would like you, my Dad, to do the same to me." She will be peacefully reproducing a smile on Gentil's reaction.

## The Work and the Environment

Environment is totally a part of my body. I always feel trees giving much more even comparing to what "I think I provide to them." The way I love my body I can obviously love trees and the entire environment in the same way. This can be successfully accomplished if I am peaceful. But when I am anxious, this fosters inequities.

In 2007 I had a fruit tree in my yard in Rwanda. Children from the neighborhood would come and easily rob the fruits. I didn't have money to put a fence and I decided to cut down the tree.

After passing through my inquiry process, I always wonder if that decision was a peaceful one to solve that problem. Furthermore, we started begging fruits from the neighbors. If I could have had The Work wakefulness, to go inside me back then and question my mind before cutting it, the tree could have been saved.

It is very difficult to protect the environment while we are stressful. It is by questioning our mind that we can know what to do.

I know this story which happened in my community. Two ladies lost their husbands and became widows.

The first widow decided to cut down all the trees on their farm because her husband was much attached to trees. The rationale behind that action was, "*When she sees the trees in their farm, she remembers the death of her husband and starts grieving.*"

The second widow, whose husband was also much attached to trees, decided to plant many trees in tribute to her husband. The rationale behind that action was, "*When she sees the trees on her farm, she remembers how her husband loved the trees and feels peaceful.*" They were both advised by their minds and "They believed that."

I met a friend in Vermont and we were discussing the massive destruction of the environment that is going on in different parts of the world. I wanted to know his contribution to save the life of this lovely environment. He told me that he has been awakened and decided to take some measures that can help him protect the environment.

He said, "I stopped camping." I wanted to know if he took that decision peacefully! He said that he found that a way to protect the environment. He asked me what I thought about his decision. I said, I would question my mind and see if, "going camping abuses the environment" then I am sure, I can decide to have one hundred saplings and during my camping time I plant them.

### Green and My Life

*No one can ignore how magic, spectacular, miraculous, trees are.*
*They do not rely on their worst experiences*
*and always they smile to me.*
*Despite our past inappropriate behavior, where we*
*destroyed billions and billions of its families, the trees*
*continue to smile to us, providing their beauty faces.*
*They always grow forth to remain much more*
*useful to us, giving us a good example of Dynamic*
*Shift Solutions by living "The Present."*
*I can also live "The Present," not relying on the past,*
*despite its status, there is always an opportunity for a*
*dynamic shift to peace for me in each moment.*

—Costa, *during a Spiritual walk conducted by Laura*
*K. Greiner, PII Greenville SC, USA, 2010*

## The Work and Religion

Does The Work relate to a religion? That is the question I have been asked by many of my community members. I was expecting this question, which I asked myself several times. More than 90% of my community members are Christian.

My answer was: "After my second School for The Work, I understood how much I have to respect God. I noticed that because I was feeling peace in me. When I was full of hatred, I was out of God's will." I do believe that God doesn't want us to suffer. But we are dumping ourselves in sufferings from our stressful stories. God's words are about The Work.

God looks beyond our stressful stories to the truth; if so, what happens to all our sins (results of our fearful minds)? By our fearful minds, we are full of resentment. If we don't question our minds, we always fall into mistakes. With our fearful minds, we reject or misinterpret the word of God. With fear comes nothing good—we suffer!

I was dodging the word of God because of my fear. All temptations were creations of my mind.

> *12 Blessed is the man who endures temptation; for when he has been approved, he will receive the crown of life which the Lord has promised to those who love Him. 13 Let no one say when he is tempted, "I am tempted by God"; for God cannot be tempted by evil, nor does He Himself tempt anyone. 14 But each one is tempted when he is drawn away by his own desires and enticed. 15 Then, when desire has conceived, it gives birth to sin; and sin, when it is full-grown, brings forth death. —*
> Holy Bible NKJV James 1:12-15

We think much more about tomorrow, but God focuses on relationship with today. When we were starving in Congo, my mom could easily tell us that God left us and remained hopeless.

Every time she would say, "Tomorrow we will be having a severe hunger," everyone would start to cry.

> *Do Not Worry²⁵ Therefore I say to you, do not worry about your life, what you will eat or what you will drink; nor about your body, what you will put on. Is not life more than food and the body more than clothing? …Now if God so clothes the grass of the field, which today is, and tomorrow is thrown into the oven, will He not much more clothe you, O you of little faith?*
>
> *³¹ Therefore do not worry, saying, 'What shall we eat?' or 'What shall we drink?' or 'What shall we wear?'…. ³⁴ Therefore do not worry about tomorrow, for tomorrow will worry about its own things. Sufficient for the day is its own trouble.* —Holy Bible NKJV Matthew 6: 25-31

We are much ruled by our fearful minds, which creates daydreams in our lives. One day I visited my friends in their home in Northeast of Bujumbura. When I was there a war started between the Hutu rebel groups and the government army. I bowed and started to pray. All the family members there were Christians. There was a massive exchange of fire bluster. Many Tutsis in the area were killed since the Hutus were dominating that area. The friends' family was Congolese and seemed to be a pro-Hutus' rebel group.

I kept praying for my God to save me. I was full of fear. The family got into a deep dispute. One part decided to chase me out of their house fearing that if the rebels came there and asked for identifications, it would be easily known from my name that I am a Rwandan and all the family will be killed. The tension of the war increased higher and higher. There were persistent severe bomb detonations. They were in total confusion and remained without a solution. I couldn't go outside because all the area was covered with the dead, full of corpses.

Three children from that family were my close friends and defended my case. Their mom loved me kindly as well. The rest of the family was against the idea of continuing to hold me there. One of the children came in the room where I was meditating with my prayer, and he said, "We are all going to be killed because of you. Stop praying and think about that!" It was by chance that the government soldiers came and surrounded all the area and looked for a corridor for us to join the peaceful areas, and then escorted us to a safe place. In our minds, that family and I were already dead before even being killed. Where was the battle? God isn't hopeless; "I" am hopeless conducted by my fear.

> *"The only thing the devil can get from you is what you hand to him. Your greatest problem isn't outside; it's within you."* —Pastor Stearns Philip Sr., Apostolic Faith Temple, Portland Maine

Before I dedicate to all readers the following poem, which is my inspiration, I will conclude for this moment by saying, "We have power inside us to control our minds. When we fail, the blame isn't to God or to someone else. With fear, we don't comprise our full being. How to discover that? We must question our stressful feelings and find out the truth. Do The Work!

### Conception-Completion-Domino Effect
### (Poem to Friends of The Work)

*Oh! "I" you have been a slave of my mind for a long time,*
*My mind told you to hate, you thought you hated,*
*You hated yourself, because you were the one who was grieving,*
*My mind conceived fear, you "I" lives stressfully!*
*"Love and Peace, are there within you,"*
*Brenda B. Good said to you!*
*Peace and Love are in me.*
*Oh! "I" what did you get from stress completion?*
*My mind could even remind you, always,*
*"There is the inner peace!"*
*The domino effect was a heartbroken life and self-destruction!*
*My "I" agreed with my mind and I lived in confusion!*
*Under a rain shower in Rwanda, Christina Syndikus invited you!*
*"Revenge is all about fear, stress, anxiety and not peace!"*
*Oh! You showed me a wrong way to be self-esteemed!*
*Through The Work I know what you meant by that!*
*The truth was released from sorrowful chains!*
*Live free! And live free! And live free! And live free!*
*Isabelle Stahl, reminded you that, "Queen Byron has no story,"*
*And she is producing smiles to everyone! Smiling machine!*
*Oh! My mind, you open the space of love in my family,*
*Pamela Grace could make mud bricks after The Work,*
*Richard Cohen and Jon Newbill shared a small bed in my house!*
*"Do The Work on that," repeatedly said Paige Tuhey.*
*I knew with The Work, we can share even the impossible!*
*And easily substitute anger with Love! I feel my inner peace!*

*Oh! My mind, don't you think that it's*
*time to focus on The Present?*
*I know tomorrow will be too late to make my peace!*
*Past years, last month and yesterday have gone forever!*
*Oh! My mind, you are no longer my fear-bearer, you are my love!*

*This is a peaceful time, Jenny O'Connor frequently mentioned!*
*This is my time, I have to welcome and enjoy as it is!*
*The best time of my life is this. This is*
*"The present" and I celebrate.*
*Costa's Inspiration*

# Acknowledgments and Gratitude

First of all, I thank God for having connected me to *The Work Of Me* that helps me days and nights to live in the harbor of peace.

I am also thankful to my country Rwanda, which after the 1994 Tutsis' Genocide has been a peaceful bay, where people can easily learn all about forgiveness and reconciliation which promote daily sustainable development. Especially my gratitude goes to His Excellence Paul Kagame, the President of Rwanda, who tremendously supports Peace, Unity, and Reconciliation among Rwandans after the 1994 Tutsis' Genocide and brings the country among the top safe ones on the planet.

From the bottom of my heart, I would like to express a word of thanks to people and organizations who contributed to this book creation.

Among them:

My wife Bernadette, my Mother Martha, my siblings, and my children Gentil, Queen Byron, Yves and Denise: You are always my love and I am to me. Your peaceful life is the result of The Work.

My community in Burundi, DRC and Rwanda: You are lovely. Marion McGillivray, her Husband Keith, and their daughter Genevieve Shill: you have been the smooth and safe "bridge" between me and The School for The Work.

Jill Fox Caruthers and Jon C. Fox, my host in Beverly Hills and in Nevada City: Your care to me was just preparing the fantastic moment of "The inquiry." You are who I am. I Love you.

Forest Charter School, Nevada City, California, thank you for having been my host. It was a peaceful memorable time. You just give what you have to the students. That is Love!

Byron Katie: You helped me to discover both fear and peace in me.

Dr. Jim Lockard, Sir: your encouragement led me to the achievement.

Center for Spiritual Living, Simi-Valley: you allow me to be part of you by giving the opportunity to sow my love.

Dr. Joel M. Rothaizer "ASHOKA" and Padamaja, MCC Clear Impact Consulting Group, Inc. Edmonton, Canada. The love you showed me toward my work increased my personal commitment of living peacefully. Clear Impact Consulting Group is a blessing to me and to all companies that host your presence.

Pastor Phillip J. Stearns Sr. from Faith Temple, Portland, Maine: your teaching carries me in a deepened spiritual life and always allows me to know that the "battlefield is in me." I love you.

Rev. Joseph Harerimana from Horebu Church: Thank you for showing me how my spiritual life is important to me.

Mediation and Restorative Justice Centre, Edmonton, Canada: Thanks for the peaceful program and for allowing me to share with you *The Work That Brings Peace in Me.*

Laura K. Greiner: You are an angel; the spiritual walk in Greenville, South Carolina, has been a great pathway of peace that opened my mind to the world of green.

Pamela Grace, Isabelle Stahl, Paige Tuhey, Brenda Becker Goodell, Christina Syndikus, Jennifer O'Connor, Richard L. Cohen, and Jon Newbill: You left everything from your homes and committed to spend days with my family and my community. Your love was welcomed as "Milk and honey."

Kari May and Lindsey May Read: you built my family and community love conviction.

Groundwork Opportunities' volunteers who spent days in my home, namely Bartlomiej Jan Skorupa, Ryan Gilpin, Kyle Miller, Sarah Sowden, Ryan and Karen Buxton, Vanessa Sloan:

Your support was the success of my commitment. You are gift of changes.

Brenda Colleen Lowe from The One Person Project, (TOPP): when you hosted me in your house in Summerland, British Columbia, and organized my presentation to Penticton community, I felt how generous Penticton Community and You in particular when you mean Peace and Love are. The tour around the First Nations communities, ten hours' drive to and from the University of British Columbia in Vancouver revealed your gratis mind of doing things. Your team is making a difference in Rwanda and Tanzania by sharing the deep peace from the hearts of your community members.

Emily and James Goodman family in Malibu, California: I thank you for having hosted me in your house and contributing to my trip of extending and strengthening my "Love."

My friend Janine Giles Canmore, Alberta, Canada, and Carrie Dustan H. Hlady from *the friendly city* Moose Jaw, Saskatchewan, Canada: Our friendship always reminds me how much the universe is lovely.

Enfield family (Tyler and Leala): I thank you for having granted the space to spread my love. What you are doing is just about love. You are a gift not only for the Edmonton community but for the entire world. I love you.

Renée Vaugeois from Ainembabazi Children's project: when you shared with me your commitment to provide love to vulnerable children in Africa, I noticed that when "I have love, I can share lovely." You are an inspiration.

Lisa Daley: When you talked to me, I always saw vital inputs to my book inspiration. You are a pure gift.

Carl Van Rossum, Mary Hicks, and Sid: Your teaching and compassion will be always in my mind. I was lucky to meet you and so are all Community in North America.

Naren King and Sono King: When we met at The School for The Work with Byron Katie in Los Angeles, you helped me to know much my "I." Sono you told me that, "Costa, you deserve peace." I love you both.

All Native Americans, African Americans, Jewish and newcomer communities I met: You showed me how much your love is in you and I love you.

New England Pachamama Alliance: you helped me to go deeper and see how social justice is part of my daily duties to live with. You enabled me to get in the family of the blue loons and share together the peaceful moment.

Eloise from New Jersey: I have harvested love from you and you are still lovely.

School for The Work: You were a peaceful lake where my stressful stories were cleaned.

Peter and Renuka from RedTV Canada, Calgary: Thank you for all lovely and interesting interviews. I Love you all.

Kathleen Grant, my book editor from Finland in Scandinavia: Your commitment to edit my book showed me how people are just angels. When we met on our flight on KLM, I felt peace and love the way you welcome my book inspiration. The connection Amsterdam-Los Angeles was a gift to me to share together The Work of Byron Katie and its impact toward self-reconciliation. Thank you for your love.

To me: I Love me. —**Costa N. Ndayisabye**

## *"Make your love and we will follow"*

*(Katie addressed this to Costa after the graduation ceremony in March 2009 School for The Work.)*

# About the Author

Costa's parents fled a Tutsis' massacre in Rwanda to Burundi in 1959. He was born in Burundi, and grew up in The Democratic Republic of Congo. In his childhood, Costa was a victim of malnutrition. After his mother widowed at a young age, he and his siblings grew up in extreme poverty. Costa was imprisoned three times, in Congo and Burundi at the age of seventeen, and in Rwanda. The family repatriated to Rwanda in 1995 after the Tutsis' Genocide, which took the lives of almost one million innocents within a period of one hundred days.

Inspired by The School for The Work with Byron Katie (www.thework.com), where he graduated twice and found out the true line of his inner-peace, Costa became an International Presenter and Facilitator for individual healing and interpersonal reconciliation. *The Work That Brings Peace in Me*—the name of his book and of his presentation—teaches much how to live The Present by questioning our mind.

"Costa's 'teaching' is so powerful and memorable because quite simply he teaches by example. He is simply living, loving, being and doing what he knows is the best and the kindest way for him in this world, regardless of personal cost or apparent risk. In tiny every day ways and in large life-changing ways he lives his "turn-arounds," and if you ask—and sometimes even if you don't—he will invite you to do the same. He has taught me so much about trust. Everywhere he goes, people are inspired. His natural goodness inspires generosity in heart after heart. Miraculously this allows him to dedicate himself full time to the service of others with even less, whether it's finding an appropriate family and home for an orphan, building a house for a displaced family, or doing the Work with his community, or meeting different communities in North America. He is invited and inspires. Those who cross his path are truly blessed. I am delighted that through reading this book, you will become one of those blessed with knowing him. —*Isabelle Stahl. Edmonton AB, Canada* (www.kindmind.ca).

# About Great Life Press

Great Life Press LLC is a new publishing company whose beginning was greatly inspired by Costa's story, and the wish to help spread his peaceful message to others.

We welcomes authors with an inspiring story to contact us at:

Great Life Press LLC
191 Parsons Rd.
Rye, New Hampshire 03870   USA
on the Web at:
www.greatlifepress.com
email: books@greatlifepress.com